DARK SKIES

*The Official Guide
to the First TV Series*

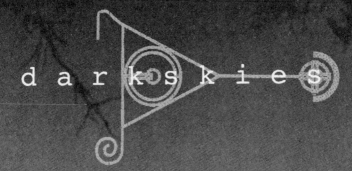

DARK SKIES

The Official Guide to the First TV Series

CHRIS BYMAN

Hodder & Stoughton

The photographs on pages 13, 14, 21, 24, 33, 41, 50,
56, 72, 84, 89, 103, 107, 141 and 169 appear with the
permission of Corbis-Bettmann/UPI.

First published in Great Britain in 1997
by Hodder and Stoughton
A division of Hodder Headline PLC

British Library Cataloguing in Publication Data
A CIP catalogue record for this title is available
from the British Library

ISBN 0 340 70784 4

Designed by Peter Ward
Printed and bound in Great Britain by
Scotprint Limited, Scotland

Hodder and Stoughton
A division of Hodder Headline PLC
338 Euston Road
London NW1 3BH

LIST OF CONTENTS

INTRODUCTION 7

"My name is John Loengard.
I am recording this because
we may not live through the
night. They're here, they're hostile
and powerful people don't want you to know.
History as we know it is a lie..."

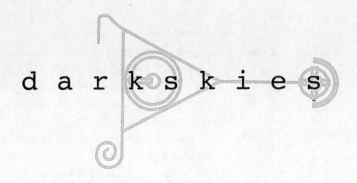

INTRODUCTION

"Imagine aliens invaded America in 1947. Imagine everything you know about history is a lie."

That's the frightening thought that John Loengard finds himself facing in 1961 when he stumbles upon a top secret United States Air Force Investigation into UFOs.

Idealistic UCLA graduate Loengard and his girlfriend Kimberley Sayers left California for Washington DC to be part of John F. Kennedy's *New Frontier* when the Democratic Senator became the United States' youngest ever President in January 1961. Like many of their generation, Loengard and Sayers were inspired by Kennedy's inaugural address, in which he asked "ask not what your country can do for you; ask what you can do for your country". Kennedy's *New Frontier* promised better things for all with its programme of civil rights measures and social reform. Loengard and Sayers were keen to make a contribution to the mood of change in their world. The last thing they expected was that they would end up leading the battle to save it.

Their problems began when Loengard found himself assigned to investigate *Project Blue Book*, a small government agency set up to monitor unexplained phenomena such as UFOs. *Project Blue Book* had been earmarked for the chop in

 The creators of *Dark Skies*, Bryce Zabel and Brent V Friedman, got much of their inspiration for the series from their timeline of events in world history set against chronologically corresponding instances of the unexplained. Here, we lay out a few of the events which might have appeared on that timeline so that you can see the connections for yourself.

a cost-cutting exercise initiated by Loengard's employer, Fresno's Congressman Pratt. However, during the course of his work on *Blue Book*, Loengard discovered that the ineffectual little project was in fact a cover for a mysterious covert agency which held evidence of the existence of an alien race far more convincing than *Project Blue Book's* fuzzy photographs and muddled testimonies. In fact, this covert agency actually had the body of an extraterrestrial held frozen in a vault below Congress. The agency was the sinister *Majestic-12*, who were to become Loengard's bitter opponents in his fight to bring to light the fact that aggressive aliens known as the "Hive" had already started to infiltrate the human race.

When, shortly after he made his startling discovery, Loengard's girlfriend Sayers became the victim of alien abduction and implantation, Loengard was left with no choice but to take upon himself the task of saving the world. For how could the human race survive if it wasn't even allowed to know its enemy?

Bryce Zabel and Brent Friedman, writers of *Dark Skies*, describe their creation as an unusual and often terrifying "blend of fact, informed speculation and dramatic license". *Dark Skies* originated when Zabel and Friedman delved into the world of UFO mythology and asked themselves how the reams of information collected by witnesses over the centuries fitted together as a whole. From the evidence they found, they created an 85 page long timeline with two columns. In the first column they put the dates of major events in world history. In the second, corresponding instances of the unexplained. This speculative timeline project soon threw up some surprising results.

Events you wouldn't normally group

1,500 BC, Egypt
In Egypt, Pharaoh Thutmose III reported seeing silent, foul-smelling circles of fire and flying discs in the sky.

600BC
The prophet Ezekiel reported the following incident by the river Chebar in the land of the Chaldeans:
    ...And I looked and behold a whirlwind came out of the north, a great cloud and a fire unfolding itself, and a brightness were about it, and out of the midst thereof as the colour of amber, out of the midst of the fire... came the likeness of four living creatures. And this was their appearance; they had the likeness of a man. And everyone had four faces and everyone had four wings... when the living creatures went, the wheels went by them; and when the living creatures were lifted up from the Earth the wheels lifted up.

100 BC, Alaska
A tribe of Tlinglit Indians camping near what was later to become Chilliwack, Alaska, witnessed the falling to earth of what they assumed to be a star. Riding on the tale of the star was a creature, "the Father", who begged them to guard the star where it had fallen until such time as it "sang its song".

together began to take on new meanings and relationships, and Zabel and Friedman found that they had unwittingly created a new view of world history. Suddenly the inexplicable could be explained, if you were prepared to accept that the human race is not alone in the universe and that the "little green man" of UFO mythology might in fact be a member of a far more technologically-advanced and aggressive race than our own. A technologically-advanced and aggressive race with designs on Planet Earth . . .

800 A.D., Peru Structures believed to be aerial landing strips were built in the Peruvian Andes. Incredible patterns were found near the city of Nazca in Peru, covering a stretch of plain a mile wide and thirty-seven miles long. The patterns had been made by the careful removal of the top level of stones on the plain, and the straight lines involved were amazing in their accuracy. The patterns were only visible in completion from the sky.

To tell the story of their new version of twentieth century world history, Zabel and Friedman created John Loengard and Kim Sayers, founders of *Dark Skies* – a grass roots movement of people who know the truth about the aliens who walk among them and who take it upon themselves to reveal the hidden danger that Majestic-12 wants to keep quiet in the interest of "National Security". Some of the characters and events which appear in the series are obviously real: President Kennedy and his assassination in Dallas, J. Edgar Hoover, Chief Justice Earl Warren and the Warren Commission, Martin Luther King Jr. and the March on Washington. As for some of the less familiar faces? Well, turns out that they might just have been real people too. Judge for yourself the truth about *Dark Skies* . . .

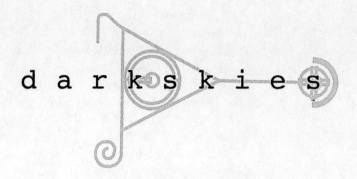

darkskies

SEASON ONE
PROGRAMME OUTLINES
Episodes One to Twelve

EPISODE ONE
The Awakening
(2 hour pilot)

WRITERS
Bryce Zabel & Brent V Friedman

DIRECTOR
Tobe Hooper

GUEST STARS
(all episodes star Eric Close as John Loengard, Megan Ward as
Kimberley Sayers and J.T.Walsh as Captain Frank Bach).

Hertzog	:	Robin Gammell
Elliot Grantham	:	G D Spradlin
Betty Hill	:	Lee Garlington
Popejoy	:	Scott Allan Campbell
Nelson Rockefeller	:	Paul Gleason
Steele	:	Tim Kelleher
Simonson	:	Francis Guinan
Barney Hill	:	Basil Wallace
Pratt	:	John M. Jackson

May 1 1960, 60,000 feet over Peshawar, West Pakistan, pilot Francis Gary Powers is flying his high-powered U-2 jet in pursuit of an even faster-moving glowing object. Through his communications radio, Powers, code-name "Talon", warns the operations crew that he is about to overfly Soviet airspace. Captain Frank Bach takes up control at this point and despite the concerns of Allen Dulles, head of the Central Intelligence Agency, that if Powers flies into Soviet airspace he could put the upcoming Summit meeting in jeopardy, Bach authorises Powers to break the border.

Above the Soviet Union, the craft Powers is pursuing suddenly stops to hover in mid-air before it shoots straight up in "an impossible vertical ascent". Powers loses the craft on his radar screen but soon he comes face to face with something much larger. The instruments on his plane start to go crazy. The plane goes into a flat spin. Powers calls Mayday and ejects to save his life.

Eighteen months later, John Loengard and Kimberley Sayers, two recent university graduates, arrive in Washington full of idealism. Loengard has land-

PLANET EARTH TIMELINE
Inexplicable

7 August 1566, Basle, Switzerland
Many witnesses reported having seen glowing discs in the sky.

March 1716, London, England
Sir Edmund Halley, the astronomer who lent his name to Halley's comet, watched a brightly lit object hover over London for two hours.

7 September 1820, Embrun, France
A number of saucer-shaped objects were seen to fly over this small French town, changing direction in a perfect 90 degree turn without breaking formation.

ed a job as an assistant to a Congressman. Sayers plans to find work once they have settled into their new apartment. It isn't a great place but, as Loengard points out, they are lucky to get a place at all since they are "living in sin". Not for the first time, Loengard asks Sayers to marry him, but she turns him down. She is an independent woman who wants to find out who "Kim Sayers" is before she becomes "Mrs. Loengard".

At work in the Congressional Office, Loengard quickly finds out that a lot of his job involves fetching donuts. Loengard's boss is Chief Aide Mark Simonson, who in turn reports to Democratic Congressman Charles Pratt. Simonson struggles to make Pratt pay attention to the important things in life, such as the Housing Bill, while Pratt is rather more concerned as to whether or not Simonson has managed to secure tickets for the US Mint tour.

Inexplicable

1869-1870, Europe
During this period of time, there were more than 2,000 reports of strange light effects on the moon. These lights appeared sometimes alone, in circles, in lines and in triangular formations. They seemed to move as if they were signalling something.

June 1877, England
Professor H. Harrison reported seeing a light on the surface of the moon like a reflection from a moving mirror.

When Loengard helps Simonson out by taking the flak for the late delivery of a package, Simonson returns the favour by allowing Loengard to stretch himself by preparing a report for the budget sub-committee. Loengard must select one program from a long list of projects for the money-saving hit list. He begins his investigation into the merits of various schemes at Wright-Patterson Air Force Base, home of *Project Blue Book*.

Blue Book is the official military investigation into UFOs and other inexplicable phenomena. Though he is slightly amused by the idea of "flying saucers", Loengard looks into the project with an open mind and decides that he will have a better idea of Blue Book's merits if he looks into some of its more recent cases himself. Loengard's research leads him to Portsmouth, New Hampshire, home of Betty and Barney Hill. Loengard manages to talk his way into their home and listens to their convincing tale of abduction, unaware that outside the house, someone else is listening too. As Loengard drives home that night he is intercepted by a UFO of his own. This time however, it is an unmarked, black helicopter. The chopper forces Loengard off the road.

Of the four black-clad men who emerge from the chopper, one is Captain Frank Bach, the man who gave Powers permission to overfly Soviet airspace, and he is the one who gives the orders now. Loengard is robbed of the tape of his interview and warned not to pursue his investigations further. Bach ends by telling Loengard menacingly that he is "A figment of (his) imagination".

January 1878, United States
The term flying saucer was first used by a Texan farmer to describe an object he had seen floating over his farm. The term was made popular in 1948 when Kenneth Arnold described a formation of objects over the Cascade Mountains in Washington State as moving "like a saucer... if you skipped it across water".

12 August 1883, Mexico
Professor Bonilla of Zacatecas, Mexico, caught a UFO on film. Bonilla's photograph is believed to be the first ever of such a subject.

Back on Capitol Hill, Loengard enters his office to find a report, titled "Project Blue Book", lying on his desk. The report's title page says that it was written by John Loengard, but Loengard has never seen the document before. The report recommends that Project Blue Book be allowed to continue its operation. Simonson takes the report from Loengard and listens sceptically to his tale about being attacked by the men in the helicopter. He puts it down to Loengard having stumbled upon a "Black Op". An operation which is merely a means of diverting funds from the government's budget. Loengard decides that this Black Op needs further investigation.

Loengard sets to work, digging through files in the Library of Congress, old newspapers, even through the personal files of a dead soldier. He is looking for news of the man amongst his attackers who was addressed by the others as Captain. Eventually he finds a man he recognises in a memo labelled "Top Secret/Majic". It is Captain Frank Bach. That night Loengard's suspicions are confirmed when he sees a TV broadcast about the hostage swap of Lieutenant Francis Gary Powers for Colonel Rudolph Abel. Bach is at the scene. Next day, Bach is accompanying Powers again through the Halls of Congress. While Powers fends off reporters, Bach takes a cigarette break and finds himself joined by Loengard.

Inexplicable

Loengard threatens Bach with a subpoena from the US Congress and demands that he tells him what is going on. Bach is unfazed. He tells Loengard that "the truth is overrated" before grabbing for the "sub-poena" which turns out to be dry cleaning receipt. Bach starts to walk away but Loengard follows and soon Bach leads him to a secret door which takes them into the HQ of the legendary Majestic-12.

Bach tells Loengard that if he wants the truth he can have it now and takes him further into the HQ to a storage room. Once inside that room he opens his attaché case and brings out a series of photographs. They are all shots of

21 April 1897, Le Roy, Kansas, United States Alexander Hamilton, a member of Congress's House of Representatives, watched a 300-foot long craft land near his home. The craft appeared to be made of glass and was carrying six "strange beings". When Hamilton and his men tried to approach the craft, it suddenly soared up into the sky.

June 1908, Tunguska, Siberia
A mysterious fireball exploded, setting 1,200 acres of farmland on fire and creating shock waves felt as far away as China's Gobi Desert. When Russian scientists, led by Leonid Kulik, subsequently visited the site of the blast, suspecting that a meteorite had hit the earth, they found no meteorite fragments but recorded unusually high levels of radioactivity, suggesting that a crippled alien craft's nuclear reactor had exploded on impact.

UFOs, and far better than anything Loengard has seen at Project Blue Book. It quickly becomes apparent that Blue Book is just a front for Majestic-12.

Next, Bach reaches inside his shirt and pulls out what

appears to be a set of dog-tags. Instead it is a container, hiding a tiny folded foil triangle. When Bach takes the triangle out of its container it magically unfolds to a hundred times its original size and floats in the air before him. He touches it, sending it spinning around, and encourages Loengard to touch it too. Bach explains that this curious hologram-like structure was found at the scene of the Roswell crash. Bach keeps it with him to remind him of the formidable technology Majestic is up against.

Loengard assumes that Bach is referring to the Russians, to which Bach replies by pulling open a refrigerated drawer to reveal a body bag. "Does this look Russian to you?" Bach asks as he unzips the body bag to reveal the shrivelled corpse of a "Gray".

Loengard is sickened, but even more so when Bach tells him that, having seen all this, Loengard is now a member of Majestic himself, with a chance to serve his country in a way he never dreamed possible. Not that Loengard can tell Kim about this "honour". When she returns from a day working on a TV special at the White House, excited at having met Jackie Kennedy, Loengard tells her that his day has been "nothing special".

Now Loengard is on call to Majestic. Pretty soon he is taken off his job as aide to Congressman Pratt to go with Bach to investigate some weird markings in a wheatfield outside Boise, Idaho. As they hover above the site in a helicopter, they see an otherworldly pictogram of intricate design that is definitely not the work of Mother Nature. Loengard, disguised as County Extension Agent Fred Grabar, is sent to interview the farmer. Before he goes, Loengard discusses the mission with Bach. Unable to tell Sayers the truth, Loengard has told Sayers that he is in Fresno, covering up the news of Congressman Pratt's extra-marital affairs. He has told Congressman Pratt that he is attending the funeral of an uncle. Bach advises him to stick to one story in the future.

Loengard finds Grantham a difficult interviewee until he tells the farmer that he wants to look at the markings to ascertain how much compensation the government should pay him for this act of "vandalism". Grantham takes Loengard up into the field and allows Loengard to wander along the lines of the pictogram. The road which crosses the symbol is covered with a strange white powder, like ash, and a metal fence has been completely melted away. Through a hidden mic, Loengard tells Majestic that the flattened stalks appear woven together and he is just about to describe a hunk of engraved gold hidden by the wheat when Grantham gets into his truck and tries to run Loengard down.

Majestic come to Loengard's rescue quickly and drive Grantham off the road. Grantham's truck rolls and he is killed.

August 1915, Gallipoli, Turkey
World War One.
The 1st/4th
Norfolk, a regiment of the British Army, disappeared while attempting to take Hill 60 at Suvla Bay near Gallipoli. Twenty-two witnesses watched the regiment of more than 800 men march into a strange formation of lenticular clouds seen hovering over the Hill. The regiment was reported as captured but at the war's end, the Turks denied all knowledge of the missing men and no trace of them was ever found.

Grantham's body is taken to Majestic headquarters to be autopsied. Dr. Hertzog can find nothing unusual about the corpse until he removes the cranial cap to examine the farmer's brain for tumours. To Hertzog's horror he finds something unearthly embedded in Grantham's amygdala. As Hertzog pulls the thing out, at Bach's insistence, it looks like some kind of lobster crossed with a spider and fights like mad to be free before Loengard manages to trap it inside a specimen jar. Even then it cracks the glass with one of its tendrils before it can be safely stowed in a freezer.

No one knows what the creature is, but it looks chillingly similar to the thing extracted from one of the Gray's brains at Roswell. Now the question is, how many more of these creatures are there?

1917, Russia
The USSR was founded as a result of the Russian Revolution in which Lenin and his Bolsheviks overthrew the Tsarist regime.

1918, Europe
The First World War ended. Peace terms were agreed by the Versailles Peace Settlement.

1924, United States
J. Edgar Hoover was appointed as the first director of the FBI.

When he returns from the Idaho mission, Loengard finds that he has been moved to a better office. Congressman Pratt is unimpressed but tells Loengard that he cannot do anything about this sudden promotion since Loengard has been declared "untouchable" by a document which includes references to Pratt's nervous breakdown. As he leaves Loengard alone to enjoy his new room, Pratt tells him ominously, "I don't know who your friends are but there are forces out there far more powerful."

Loengard continues to lead a double life; congressional aide and Majestic agent. One night he and Agent Popejoy are left to guard a chimpanzee which has been injected with a piece of the creature pulled from Grantham's brain. Since nothing much seems to be happening, Loengard continues to work on his profile of "Patient Zero", Elliot Grantham, who, according to his friends, had a missing time gap, just like Betty and Barney Hill.

Popejoy falls asleep and when Loengard next looks up from his books, the chimpanzee is no longer in its cage.

9 May 1926, North Pole
Rear Admiral Richard E Byrd made his first exploratory flight over the North pole.

1927-34, United States/Europe
Radio signals were received from the direction of the moon.

29 November 1929, South Pole
Rear Admiral Byrd made an exploratory flight over the South pole.

When Loengard goes into the lab to try to recapture the chimp, he sees that the chimp has managed to open the complicated lock on the cage door. While he is pondering this, the chimp swings down from the ceiling to attack him. Loengard is knocked out, and when Popejoy comes to his rescue, the chimp knocks him out with a piece of piping before firing on him with his own gun. Popejoy is dead before other cloakers can capture the chimp.

1930, United States
General MacArthur became the US Army Chief of Staff.

While Loengard is fighting implanted monkeys, Sayers goes to find him at his Congressional Office. Loengard is not there of course, but Congressman Pratt is and he is rifling through Loengard's papers. When Sayers confronts him, Pratt suggests that they compare stories on Loengard's whereabouts during the week when he says he went to Fresno. They come up with different stories of course and Sayers returns to the apartment determined to confront Loengard about his lies.

Loengard cannot bring himself to explain Majestic and walks out into the night to avoid confrontation. Sayers goes to bed alone. However, she is soon awakened by a strange hum. The doors and window to her room are open. Getting out of bed to close them, she is horrified to discover that she is not alone any more.

Spindly, hunched forms step forward from every corner. As they move into the light, it becomes clear that they are creatures like the one stored in Majestic's secret vault – they are Grays. One of them pinches off the end of an organic looking pod and pours out a strange green fluid. The fluid seeps towards Sayers and soon starts to spread up her body, immobilising her in a sticky opaque film. Her scream frozen with her body, Sayers is taken out of her room and into the light of a waiting craft.

PLANET EARTH TIMELINE
Inexplicable

28 December 1933, Sweden
The Swedish Flying Corps began an investigation into unidentified flying objects that had been crossing their airspace. Major General Reuterswaerd reported that: "there can be no doubt about illegal air traffic over our secret military areas. There are many reports from reliable people which describe close observation of the enigmatic flier. And in every case the same remark can be noted: No insignia or identifying marks were visible... The question is, who or whom are they, and why have they been invading our air territory."

1 February 1934, London, England
Unidentified objects seen in the air over London.

The morning after, Loengard wakes to find himself on the sofa, with the debris of his rage still scattered around him. In the bedroom, he finds Sayers asleep. She wakes at his touch but complains that she still feels terribly tired. When Loengard goes to call her office and say that she will be late, Sayers sits up and notices that there is blood on her pillow. In fact, her nose is still bleeding.

Loengard goes to work as usual. For Majestic. He attends a meeting of the dozen directors of Majestic to present to them "The Monkey Film" in which the chimp kills Popejoy. Dr. Hertzog explains that they have decided to call the alien entity a "ganglion". Then Loengard goes on to explain his latest theory, that recently implanted hosts may experience emotional and intellectual scrambling due to damage to the amygdala, which controls emotional responses. This is illustrated by a film in which a female implantee gives fairly sensible answers to nonsensical questions, since she is responding to the tone and not the content of the questions. When the film is over, Bach admits that the woman has since died as the result of a surgical procedure to remove the ganglion from her brain.

Before the assembled directors can argue about the ethics of experimenting on implantees such as this housewife, Albano interrupts with an important message for Bach. As a result, Bach dismisses Hertzog and Loengard so that the directors can continue the board meeting in secret.

That night, Loengard finds Sayers in a crowd of people outside a television store, watching President Kennedy delivering a speech to the nation. The speech seems to be making no sense to Kim but a fellow onlooker tells Loengard that America is about to go to war. The Soviets have got missiles in Cuba.

Loengard hurries straight to Bach's home to find out how much he knows. Loengard cannot understand why Kennedy and Krushchev are arguing over Cuba when the Patient Zero discovery has uncovered a far greater threat to humanity. Bach tries to dismiss Loengard but Loengard persists until he finds out that Kennedy doesn't even know about Majestic, let alone the ganglion. Bach justifies his actions by pointing at the chaos the Cuban crisis is already causing. The possible presence of aliens would surely cause a far worse outbreak of panic.

11 June 1934, London, England More unidentified craft seen over London. A report by the Royal Air Force stated that while night flying was "frequently practised" pilots were forbidden to take their planes over London at less than 5,000 ft. The identity of the craft flying low over London was "not officially known".

Loengard goes home to comfort Kim, but she already has a visitor. It is Congressman Pratt, come to tell her that she must keep an eye on Loengard so that one day she can experience the "joy of singularity". While he is talking to her, Pratt produces a globe of light and encourages Sayers to touch it. They are interrupted just in time by Loengard.

Pratt claims that he is there to discuss Cuba but Sayers is railing about something inside her head and Loengard realises she may be talking about a ganglion. Loengard flies at Pratt and they fight until Pratt stumbles backwards and falls out of the high window onto the street below. Loengard leaves in the confusion that follows. He needs to get Sayers to Hertzog as quickly as possible so that they can perform their experimental alien ejection technique, the ART.

Hertzog refuses to perform the ART himself but gives Loengard the necessary chemicals. Loengard drives Sayers to a deserted house, where he forces her to drink the chemicals which will alter the PH level in her body and force the ganglion out. After that, he administers an injection of acetone. When Sayers becomes violent, Loengard straps her to a chair until eventually, she spits the ganglion out and Loengard crushes the creature to death with his shoe.

When Loengard then carries an unconscious Sayers back out to the car, Majestic are already waiting. They insist that Sayers must be taken in for observation. She is clear of the ganglion, but her experience has made Loengard determined

to quit Majestic. Bach won't hear of such a thing so Loengard has to formulate a plan to force Majestic out into the open.

With Sayers posing as a schoolteacher to distract Mrs. Bach's attention, Loengard climbs into Bach's house and steals the artefact from Bach's locket while he is in the shower. Then, using Sayers' contacts at the White House, Loengard ensures that the artefact, along with a signed affidavit, finds its way into the hands of President Kennedy himself.

Three days later, Loengard is summoned to meet another Kennedy, Robert, the Attorney General, at his Hickory Hill mansion. On the instructions of the President, Robert asks Loengard to be the President's insider at Majestic. At Majestic headquarters, Bach hears every word of the conversation but he is confused as to why the President is taking Loengard so seriously... Until he opens his locket and discovers that the tiny container is empty.

When Loengard returns to his apartment, it has been ransacked, and Majestic agents are waiting in the shadows to take him out too. However, Loengard and Sayers manage to escape and flee for their lives. They next stop at a hotel outside Norman, Oklahoma, jumping each time the doorbell rings. But Majestic haven't caught up with them yet. It is just the manager of the motel. Crying bitterly, she tells them to turn on their TV. When they do, Sayers and Loengard hear the terrible news that President Kennedy is dead.

Sayers and Loengard hit the road again. Sayers is convinced that the President was killed because he knew about Majestic, but Loengard reassures her that his death will not be in vain, because they still have the truth on their side.

MUSIC

Stand by Me by Ben E King
Runaway by Del Shannon
Mack the Knife by Bobby Darrin

See:
Bach — The Monkey Film — A.R.T. — Loengard
Lee Harvey Oswald — Chesney — Sayers — Majestic-12
E.B.E Profile — Cuban Missile Crisis
Francis Gary Powers — Major Robert Friend
Kennedy, John F. — Betty and Barney Hill
Project Blue Book — Kennedy, Jackie
Kennedy, Robert F — Krushchev — Crop Circles
Patient Zero (Elliot Grantham) — Hertzog, Carl
Marcel, Jesse — The Monkey Film — Halligan, Charles
Organic Freeze Orbs — Popejoy — Roswell Incident
Simonson, Mark — Steele — Truman — Singularity
Grays

Moving Targets

WRITERS
Bryce Zabel & Brent V Friedman

DIRECTOR
Thomas J Wright

GUEST STARS
Terry Bozeman
Jack Lindine
Richard Fancy
Conor O'Farrell
Richard Gilliland
Hansford Rowe
Mary Kay Adams
Leon Russom
Steele : Tim Kelleher
James F Kelly
Charley Lang

CO-STARRING

Base Commander	:	Brad Blaisdell
Clark Balfour	:	Stephen James Carver
Cop	:	William Frankfather
Clint Hill	:	Brent Huff
Jackie Kennedy	:	Locky Lambert
Corporal	:	Ashley Smeck
Ground Control Worker	:	Andrew Walker

Roswell Air Force Base, July 2, 1947. A young Lieutenant Commander Frank Bach is amongst US troops awaiting the arrival of a "ship" that has requested a time and location to land at the United States only nuclear base. President Truman is also there, ready to greet the visitors who arrive not from overseas but from outer space.

Sixteen years later, just outside Norman, Oklahoma, Kimberley Sayers watches as John Loengard fires the first of several gunshots into the chassis of their '57 Chevy Bel Air.

Sayers remembers the day that Loengard bought the car, but now she knows that it must be dumped, riddled with bullet holes and smeared with blood from a cut on Loengard's finger, to make Loengard and Sayers' pursuers believe that they are dead.

At Andrews Air Base later that afternoon, Captain Bach is among those inspecting the casket containing the body of newly assassinated President Kennedy. Bach is just about to inspect the suit JFK was wearing when he was shot when he is interrupted by a petite brunette. She is Jackie Kennedy, the president's beautiful young widow, who cannot understand the importance of Bach's investigation because she does not know about Majestic or their suspicions that JFK's death may have more sinister implications than anyone could possibly imagine. Jackie Kennedy wants Bach out of the way but by the time he is dismissed by the Attorney General, Bobby Kennedy, Bach has already seen enough to say, "If he had the item, he left it in Dallas."

Meanwhile Loengard calls Bobby Kennedy, who reveals that the "evidence" that Majestic are looking for is indeed still in Dallas. Bobby Kennedy knows that his brother passed the "artefact", which Loengard stole from Bach, to someone else for safe-keeping before he took that fateful drive.

1935, United States
Scientists Van der Pol and Stormer detected radio signals from the moon.

13 August 1936, Sweden
A Swedish Air Force pilot encountered a "dark, cigar-shaped flying object about 50 ft long and 3 feet in diameter flying at 400 miles an hour". The object had no wings and no rudder.

Loengard goes to Fort Worth in Texas to meet the man now in possession of the most important piece of evidence in the fight to bring the existence of aliens to light. Loengard uses the code words "Dark Skies" to gain an audience with Jesse Marcel, a retired military man who was present at Roswell during the incident of July 1947. While Loengard talks to Marcel, Majestic are on a wild goose chase in the hotel room where Kennedy spent his last night. Agent Steele takes scissors to the upholstery in an attempt to find the cigarette lighter containing the artefact which Marcel now shows Loengard in another room in another hotel.

Marcel reveals that Kennedy was planning to get together a group of people from the military and NASA to come forward with the truth in front of the whole nation. While Marcel explains the story, Loengard flicks open the lighter to release the triangular shaped hologram which used to hang around Captain Bach's neck.

Suddenly, a flashback to Roswell. A single Gray has been sent down from the visiting ship to deliver a message to President Truman. Marcel tells Loengard that it was beautiful, like an angel. When the Gray leaves however, a visibly shaken President orders that the ship be shot out of the sky as it attempts to take off, and that any surviving Grays be taken into captivity.

Waiting outside the hotel where Loengard is meeting Marcel, Sayers sees a Majestic operative and calls Loengard in Marcel's room to let him know he may be in danger. Moments later, Majestic storm Marcel's room but Loengard has already slipped away via the fire escape with the artefact in his possession. Marcel is taken in for questioning at Majestic Headquarters.

Later that night, outside a seedy joint in Dallas called "Carousel Club", known to Loengard and Sayers as a Majestic front, Majestic Agent Steele is keeping a rendezvous with a police car. The driver of the car hands over three rifle shells which Steele takes with him when he pays a visit on the night club's owner, Jack Ruby. Ruby is found doodling Hive glyphs on a serviette and complains of hearing things, suggesting that he has been recently implanted. Round-faced Ruby was once a good time guy but now Steele is making life very difficult for him.

Steele takes Ruby into his office, which is plastered with pictures of JFK, and tells him that he wants him to kill Lee Harvey Oswald, the man being held for the assassination.

PLANET EARTH
TIMELINE
Inexplicable

25 February 1942, Los Angeles, United States
Unidentified flying objects were seen over Los Angeles soon after the Pearl Harbour incident, prompting a massive air strike against them, lest they be Japanese. Strangely, the largest of the objects remained stationary while it was being fired upon. Later it was officially reported that the barrage of fire had been an over-excited response to a false alarm, but a memo from General George C. Marshall, Chief of Staff, to President Franklin D. Roosevelt suggests otherwise when it reports that "Unidentified airplanes, other than American Airforce or Naval Planes were probably over LA... As many as fifteen airplanes may have been involved, flying at various speeds from 'very slow' to as much as 200 m.p.h. and at elevations from 9,000 to 18,000 feet."

28 January 1938, Europe
Reports of an auroral display of light from the moon.

Ruby tries to wriggle out of the assignment, but Steele warns him that he has no choice. While Sayers watches the meeting from behind a door that has been left slightly ajar, Steele opens his mouth to reveal the tendrils of a ganglion, which he forces into Ruby's mouth. While Ruby recovers from the assault, Steele talks on a radio using the language of the Hive, giving Sayers conclusive evidence that Steele was implanted by a ganglion at Majestic HQ. While Sayers continues to listen, she makes out the words "Paul Fuller" and "Andrews Air Force Base."

When he hears Sayers' story, Loengard calls Bach right away to warn him that Steele is Hive and was almost definitely involved in the JFK hit. While Sayers and Loengard are standing at the phone box, a passer-by tells them that someone just shot Lee Harvey Oswald dead. Not long afterwards they discover that the assassin on this occasion was indeed Jack Ruby.

Loengard decides that Sayers should return to the White House while he flies alone to Andrews Air Base to investigate the Hive connection with Paul Fuller. Once back at the White House, Sayers quickly finds herself involved with the arrangements for JFK's funeral.

Bach has at least taken some notice of Loengard's warning about Steele. The errant officer begs to be allowed to "Take out" Loengard but instead he is taken off his duties and frog-marched to the Majestic biolab for ART. When he realises what is happening, Steele puts up a formidable fight, killing a fellow Majestic officer in the process of trying to escape the treatment that could kill the ganglion inside him. Steele manages to get out of the lab and starts running but before he can get very far, he collapses. Bach stands over him and questions him about Ruby. Bach knows that Oswald was Steele's man. He also knows that there were three shooters involved in the assassination but only Steele knows who they were.

Majestic follow Loengard to Andrews Airbase, where Loengard has just discovered that Colonel Paul Fuller is the pilot of Air Force One, the President's plane. Loengard also finds a medical record which describes a period of absence in Fuller's career as a result of a misdiagnosed brain tumour, which seems to suggest implantation. Before Loengard can find out more, he is arrested by Military Police and taken back to Majestic.

In an argument with Bach, Loengard begs to be set straight about Roswell and Bach obliges. In a flashback to the night of the Roswell Incident, the artefact's true purpose is revealed. In a tent set up near the site of the spacecraft's landing, President Truman comes face to face with the appointed messenger of the Grays. As the Grays are unable to communicate through speech, the creature sends out a hologram-like structure similar to that contained within the lighter, then beckons Truman to touch it. Hesitantly, Truman does as he is asked and discovers that the triangular structure is a communication device. Upon touching it, Truman can hear the Gray's thoughts. But the alien is thinking the last thing President Truman expects to hear. The President leaps back from the alien's communication device as if he has been burned and tells his astounded advisors: "They just demanded our unconditional surrender."

The Gray returns to his ship and Truman orders an immediate offensive on the advice of Bach who, using the Nazis as a model, figures that the Grays are bluffing. He reasons that the Grays have nothing but their aircraft since he suspects that they would have used any weapons they had. In return for his advice, Truman puts Bach in charge of all future dealings with the alien forces and Majestic-12 is born.

Bach then asks Loengard what he was doing at Andrews Air Force Base. Loengard recounts Steele's conversation with the Hive but Bach and Loengard have no clue as to the significance of Paul Fuller until Loengard calls Sayers at the White House. The itinerary for JFK's funeral includes a military flyover of fifty fighter planes and Air Force One. Hearing this, Bach decides that Paul Fuller must have been set on a suicide mission to crash his plane onto the assembled heads of nations while they are paying their respects to the dead President. Bach gets onto Fuller's case.

In the laboratory, Agent Steele suddenly awakes from his coma and breaks free of his bonds with supernatural strength. The ganglion has not been ejected. In fact, the ART experience just seems to have put Steele even more firmly under Hive control than before.

12 August 1942, Solomon Islands Sergeant Stephen J. Brickner of the US Marines reported seeing a formation of UFOs above Tulagi in the Solomon Islands.

Breaking out of the Majestic building, Steele hi-jacks a helicopter to take him to JFK's funeral. He is pursued by Loengard, who has managed to escape from his own cell in the confusion following Steele's awakening. Loengard climbs on board the chopper as it is leaving the ground and following a dramatic mid-air struggle, Steele falls to almost certain death.

When Loengard has dealt with Steele, he persuades the chopper pilot to give him a free ride to Washington, where JFK is being interred at Arlington Cemetery. John arrives just in time to see Majestic agent Albano rob Sayers of the artefact, which she has been keeping out of harm's way. Loengard goes to shoot Albano but finds himself unable to when Albano tells him that he will have to shoot his target in the back of the head if he really wants the artefact.

Far away from the funeral at Majestic HQ, Colonel Bach comforts another widow. Not Jackie Kennedy this time, but Agent Steele's wife. While she is crying, Bach is called away, only to be told by his agents that Steele's body has not been found. It seems that Majestic's very own Hive infiltrator is not quite dead.

See:

DARK SKIES: THE OFFICIAL GUIDE

EPISODE THREE
Mercury Rising

WRITER
James D Parriott

DIRECTOR
Tucker Gates

GUEST STARS
Pat Crawford Brown
Todd Jeffries
Tim Kelleher
John Mese
Glen Morshower
Natalija Nogulich
Conor O'Farrell
Peter Van Norden

CO-STARRING
Patrolman	:	Steven Barr
TV anchor	:	Don Clark
Gate Guard	:	Darryl Rocky Davis
Fisherman	:	Henry Harris
Gary Augatreux	:	Todd Jeffries
Bartender	:	George Lugg
Cloaker	:	Grant Mathis

January 30, 1964. In a roadside motel in Biloxi, Mississippi, Sayers and Loengard are catching up with the news. President Johnson and French Premier DeGaulle are at odds over Vietnam. The Winter Olympics are underway in Innsbruck, Austria. The sixth Ranger moon probe has just been launched. Will it be the first to send back pictures?

Sayers is feeling twitchy. She has an inexplicable urge to go to Florida and quickly. Loengard isn't keen. To get there by the next day, they would need to go by Interstate and that would be too dangerous. But that night, Sayers has a disturbing dream. She imagines that an astronaut in distress is lying on a bench alongside her. The astronaut reaches out to her, pleading for her help, but before Sayers can grasp his hand he disappears. Next day, Sayers' urge to go to Florida is even stronger than before.

Loengard gives in to Sayers' gut feeling and they head for Florida. Loengard drives while Sayers absentmindedly sketches on a map. Glancing at her doodles, Loengard is horrified to see that she has sketched a glyph that he remembers from Patient Zero's wheat field. When he asks Sayers why she is sketching that particular symbol, she cannot say. Loengard thinks she is hiding something and knows that they cannot move on until they have faced it together.

While they are driving a highway patrol car appears in the rear window and they get pulled over for speeding. The patrolman asks to see Loengard's license and goes to call in the details on his radio. Realising that Majestic will be able to track them from the patrolman's call, Loengard decides that his only option is to put the patrolman out of action and he backs into the patrol car to slow the policeman down before burning rubber all the way to Mobile, Alabama. Once there, Loengard tries to persuade Sayers to board a bus to Houston to put Majestic off the scent but she is still insistent that she must go to Florida. Finally she tells Loengard about the astronaut in her vision.

Meanwhile at Majestic HQ, Bach is studying a series of moon-shots. The third shot he sees seems to show a structure of some kind, a pyramid perhaps . . . Nothing that couldn't be explained as a trick of the light. Bach is interrupted by Albano, bringing news that Sayers and Loengard are en route to Florida.

Sayers and Loengard have finally reached Cape Canaveral, Florida. While Loengard signs a motel register, Sayers finds herself strangely drawn to a man pulling up outside the motel on a motorbike. Without telling Loengard, Sayers follows the mystery biker into a bar, whereupon the biker freezes, as if in recognition of her, and they clasp each other's hands. Before they have a chance to talk however, the biker is interrupted by

PLANET EARTH TIMELINE
On The Record

May 1945, Europe
The Second World War ended in Europe, with Germany surrendering after its leader Adolf Hitler committed suicide.

6 and 9 August 1945, Japan
The United States used atomic bombs against Japan in Hiroshima and Nagasaki.

September 1945, Japan
Japan surrendered, bringing the Second World War to a close. Fifteen million military personnel had been killed over six years of fighting, including two million Soviet prisoners of war. The death toll for civilians was estimated at thirty-five million. The USA and the Soviet Union emerged from the wreckage of the war as the two largest world powers.

his friend, "Gator", who has come to collect him accompanied by two of the notorious "Men in Black". Once the mystery man has left, Sayers explains to Loengard that she thinks he was the astronaut in her dream. That they are connected in some way is confirmed by the hastily scribbled note the astronaut left behind upon which Loengard recognises the Hive Glyph.

Back in Alabama, the patrolman who stopped Loengard and Sayers is showing an interested visitor their abandoned car. It is Steele, the ex-Majestic agent Loengard hoped he had killed by pushing him out of a helicopter. In the car's pocket, Steele finds the map of Florida onto which Sayers drew the Hive

On The Record

1945, Vietnam
Vietnam became independent from France.

1945, United States The United Nations was formed in San Francisco, replacing the League of Nations as the premier international organisation working for world peace and security.

glyph. Her doodle is placed right over the town of Cape Canaveral.

Loengard is unconvinced that Sayers should meet the astronaut that night as suggested by his note. If Sayers thinks that she first encountered the astronaut while she was being abducted by the Grays, then it stands to reason that the astronaut was also implanted and it is unlikely that he has undergone ART since. Sayers overrides Loengard's uneasiness and they meet the astronaut regardless. His name is Ty Yount and he says that he has been seeing Sayers in his dreams for some time. He tells Loengard and Sayers that he is an astronaut from "Midnight Wing", a covert arm of NASA.

PLANET EARTH
TIMELINE
Inexplicable

1946, World-wide, especially Scandinavia
During this year there were more than 2,000 sightings of "ghost rockets" seen as far afield as Scandinavia and India. The "ghost rockets" were rocket shaped objects with fiery tails that moved at great speed.

22 August 1946, Norway
The Norwegian government censored "rocket stories" in the national press.

Encouraged by Sayers, Yount also reveals that he flew on the "unmanned" Gemini prototype which was launched on October 21st, the night that Sayers was abducted. Yount's mission was to seek and destroy a Soviet satellite known as the "Black Knight", a mission so secret that even Kennedy was in the dark about it.

When the Gemini prototype approached the "Black Knight", Yount and his co-pilot "Gator" Augatreux estimated the triangular-shaped craft to be as big as a football stadium. A space launch missile was prepared to fire upon the satellite but before that was possible, the astronauts were blinded by a bright light. When they came to, the mission clock was reading two hours later, the astronauts' craft was on the other side of earth and the "Black Knight" was gone. Augatreux thought he must have triggered the missile. Houston thought the Gemini prototype had been wiped out.

Now Yount is due to fly on the "unmanned" Saturn launch with his Gemini co-pilot Augatreux, but before he does that he wants Sayers to talk to someone for him – a hypnotist, Dr. Helen Gould, whose job is to ensure the mental health of the Midnight Wing pilots.

Dr. Helen Gould wants to regress Sayers to find out the truth behind her dream. Under hypnosis, Sayers remembers the night of her abduction. She finds herself helpless as Grays enter her bedroom and cocoon her in a green encasing fluid before she is transported to their ship. Once inside the ship, Sayers is subjected to an examination by a probing light which seems to read her mind before it is moved onto the body next to her. Sayers realises that body belongs to Ty Yount as he reaches out to her exactly as in her dream. Once again, before they can touch, Yount disappears. Voices inside Sayers' head tell her that they don't want him, they want her. Then the ultimate horror occurs and the Grays implant Sayers with a ganglion via her nose. While she is being implanted she can hear another human being screaming but is unable to see his face because he is wearing an astronaut's mask.

Even after hearing Sayers' testimonial, Yount still wants to fly and cannot be persuaded otherwise. Dr. Gould pronounces him fit and warns Loengard and Sayers to get off the base before they get into trouble.

The motel is no longer safe however, since Steele has tracked them down. He bursts into their room and shoots a body in the bed, only to discover when a woman other than Sayers walks out of the shower that he has shot the wrong man. With the emotional detachment of the Hive, Steele finishes the innocent woman off regardless.

The next day, before the launch, Bach listens to Sayers' testimonial, which was secretly recorded. Meanwhile Sayers, dozing in the car, goes one stage deeper into her dream as she realises that the screaming body she couldn't recognise before is Ty Yount's co-pilot Augatreux. She deduces from this that Augatreux must therefore have been implanted. When she tells Loengard, he calls Bach straight away to warn of the danger that the Saturn launch could be sabotaged by the Hive. Bach hangs up however, forcing Loengard to break into the launch area to underline the seriousness of his news but, even when he knows that Loengard is right beneath the rocket, Bach still refuses to stop the countdown. As far as Bach is concerned, both pilots on the Gemini mission were checked using the EBE profile and given the all clear.

Sayers and Loengard risk being fried to death in the heat

On The Record

1947, United States
President Truman became the first American president to address the nation by television.

1947, United States
The CIA, or Central Intelligence Agency, was established by Congress to control US intelligence operations both in the United States and overseas.

1947, USSR
"Cominform" was established. This alliance of communist nations had the aim of world revolution.

generated by take-off as they linger beneath the launch pad trying to explain the predicament to Bach. Finally, Bach checks the credentials of the agent who performed the EBE and realises that Loengard is right. The EBE was performed by Steele after his implantation and therefore it must have been unreliable. The countdown is stopped while Augatreux is removed from the control pod and exterminated. Though they have just saved him hundreds of millions of dollars, Bach warns Loengard and Sayers to leave straight away.

Later, the Saturn launch goes ahead with just one pilot. Yount makes contact with the Ranger probe and the first photographs of the moon are beamed back to Mission Control.

This time, the pyramid structure seen in the early photos is much, much clearer. It is the Black Knight, as seen on the Gemini mission, hovering above the surface of the moon. Bach has Mission Control closed down for debriefing. A television news broadcaster announces the news that the latest Ranger mission has failed to send back pictures once again. NASA announce that all further missions will be postponed until corrections have been made to the equipment.

PLANET EARTH TIMELINE
Inexplicable

February 1947, North Pole
Rear Admiral Byrd made another flight over the North Pole during which he made controversial comments that suggested he had in fact flown through a Polar depression and into the centre of the earth. The Press reported that members of the expedition had accomplished a flight of 2,000 miles from McMurdo Sound and penetrated a land extent of 2,300 miles beyond the Pole. To travel this far beyond the Pole without encountering the sea should have been impossible but Byrd sent back news of the "land beyond the Pole with its mountains, trees, rivers and a large animal identified as a mammoth". His seemingly fantastical reports were confirmed by the expedition's radio operator Lloyd K. Grenlie, before the New York papers reported that "a strict censorship was imposed from Washington".

MUSIC
Since I Fell For You by Lenny Welch

See:

EPISODE FOUR
Dark Day's Night

WRITERS
Brent V Friedman and Brad Markowitz

DIRECTOR
Matt Pann

GUEST STARS
Kathleen Garrett
Stanley Kamel
Tim Kelleher
Charley Lang
Conor O'Farrell
Gina Phillips

CO-STARRING

Cabbie	:	Joseph Corberry
Doorman	:	Earl Carroll
Brian Epstein	:	Carey Endel
Usher	:	John H Freeland Jr.
Michael Hagerty	:	Chris Weal
Ed Sullivan	:	Jerome Patrick Hoban
Mrs. Weatherly	:	Sandra Ellis Lafferty
Kenneth Parkinson	:	James Lancaster
Neighbour	:	Karen Maurise
Technician	:	Dominic Oliver
Ringo Starr	:	Carmine Grippo
Paul McCartney	:	Tim Michael McDougall
George Harrison	:	Richard Antony Pizaria
John Lennon	:	Joe Stefanelli

February 6th, 1964. New York City. Advertising executive Ron Burnside, of Synduct Research, drives graduate student Christopher Weatherly to a news kiosk. Weatherly has just taken part in an experiment, during which he had to watch a series of advertisements. Now Burnside wants Weatherly to go to the news kiosk and buy the first magazine which attracts his attention to complete the test. It seems an easy way for the student to earn money. As he chooses his magazine the woman working in the booth turns up her radio which is playing a Beatles song, "Money (That's what I want)". Weatherly pays for his magazine, then, inexplicably, he walks straight out into the road against a "Don't Walk" sign and is killed by a passing car. The woman from the kiosk, whose name is Donna Hargrove, joins Ron Burnside in his car.

In a motel near Savannah, Georgia, Sayers and Loengard are tracking a Hive broadcast on a ham radio set. Amongst the garbled Hive words, Sayers manages to pick out something that sounds like "1697 Broadway, Sunday", and suddenly Loengard and Sayers are going to New York.

They sell their car and fly to be able to make New York by the Sunday mentioned in the Hive message. As they arrive at Idlewild Airport, newly renamed JFK Airport in honour of the recently assassinated president, they find themselves caught up in the midst of Beatlemania. The Beatles are due to arrive in New York for their first live American appearance on the Ed Sullivan show and the airport is full of screaming fans – fortunately for Sayers and Loengard. As they are struggling through the crowds, Sayers spots Steele and creates a smokescreen by announcing that she has just seen Paul McCartney, thus sending a crowd of girls stampeding towards their enemy.

Back at Majestic HQ, Bach and Dr. Halligan are studying the ganglion extracted from the brain of Argatreux the astronaut, when Bach receives the news that Steele has been spotted in New York. Halligan has been pondering how the other astronaut on Argatreux's mission could possibly have remained unimplanted. He suggests that biological incompatibility may be the reason and demonstrates this by killing the ganglion extracted from Argatreux with an injection of the "throwback" Yount's blood.

Loengard and Sayers head for their Broadway address and discover that it is the Sullivan Theatre, home of the Ed Sullivan show. That night the Beatles are due to play their first live American gig at the theatre, and it occurs to Sayers and

Loengard that the Hive could be planning to injure the band. Loengard sneaks into the theatre to warn the Beatles' manager, Brian Epstein, to double-check his security arrangements. Epstein doesn't want to know, he is too busy arguing with Ed Sullivan, but John Lennon gives Loengard an autograph for his troubles.

Meanwhile, Sayers has tracked down the radio ham whose broadcast they picked up in Savannah. The ham's name is Christopher Weatherly. However, when Sayers and Loengard go in search of him, they discover that he died a week earlier in a strange traffic accident. Sure that the Hive has something to do with Weatherley's death, Loengard and Sayers break into his house anyway and

17 February 1947, USSR
The radio programme "Voice of America" was broadcast in Russian for the first time in an attempt to undo some of the damage done to the American image in Russia by Soviet misinformation.

discover radio equipment tuned into the channel they picked up in Georgia, along with a radio ham's log book. In Weatherly's room, Sayers also finds a flyer related to the advertising experiments. The date of the experiment, ringed in red, is the day that Weatherly died. Before they can discover more, they are interrupted by the unexpected return of Christopher's parents, and have to leave quickly, via the window. Flicking

through the log book later that night, they find the name of Ron Burnside, the experiment's organiser.

Sayers and Loengard decide to go along to the experiment themselves to find out what it is all about. In the queue of people waiting to take part, they meet a young girl trying to raise enough money for a Beatles ticket. She introduces herself as Marnie Lane.

The experiment starts, with the woman from the kiosk, Donna Hargrove, running the film of adverts on which the subjects are ostensibly to be asked to comment. While watching the adverts, Sayers experiences slight discomfort and seems to see symbols inserted into the film. Symbols that closely resemble Hive glyphs. Marnie Lane also seems to be suffering and she suddenly runs outside to get some air. Sayers follows her and discovers that Marnie has experienced similar feelings of sickness before, especially since she started having a particular dream.

The dream is always the same: Marnie is in a car with her Aunt Hazel, driving to Niagara for the weekend. They are arguing about a radio broadcast when suddenly the radio signal goes crazy and the sky is filled with a bright white light. Simultaneously, the radio aerial snaps right off the car and is whipped up into the air towards some kind of UFO. Marnie manages to get out of the car and runs into the woods but under the cover of the trees, Marnie runs straight into a creature which Sayers recognises from the description as one of the Grays.

Marnie is concerned that she is going mad but Sayers reassures her that she is quite normal. Sayers doesn't think it is a good idea to let Marnie know that she may actually have been abducted and instead sends the young girl back home on the next bus. While Sayers thinks that Marnie may have been abducted, she is sure that the girl is not Hive.

12 March 1947, United States President Truman asked for $400 million to support the stand against communism in Greece and Turkey. When justifying this donation, Truman told his Senate "I believe that it must be the policy of the US to support free peoples who are resisting attempted subjugation by armed minorities or outside pressures." Though he did not name them overtly, it was believed at the time that Truman was referring to the Soviet Union and the forces of Communism.

In a car driving back to the Ed Sullivan theatre, Sayers hears a Beatles song on the radio. It is "Money (That's what I want)" again. Sayers asks the cab driver to turn the song up and is suddenly gripped by an urge to throw herself out of the cab. When Loengard calms her down, she tells him that while the song was playing she experienced blips similar to those she saw during the advertisement trials. Sayers suggests that the Hive are using subliminal messages similar to the blipverts which were once used in cinema advertising to persuade people to buy popcorn and candy. Loengard is sceptical – he hasn't seen the blips – until Sayers explains about Marnie and suggests that only people who have been abducted are affected.

This doesn't fit with Christopher Weatherly's death. Marnie seems to have been a throwback. Sayers has been ART'd. But why would the Hive want to kill one of its own? Loengard examines the radio ham's log book again and makes the startling discovery that the Christopher Weatherly who died was not Christopher Weatherly the radio ham after all. The log book belongs to Christopher Weatherly Snr. His father. This leads

Sayers to compare the Weatherlys to the astronauts on the Gemini mission. Both were abducted, but only one was implanted.

Before Sayers and Loengard have time to reflect on this latest discovery, they are interrupted by the appearance of a figure on the fire escape of their hotel room. Loengard manages to push Sayers to the ground just before Steele fires his gun. Steele and Loengard seem to be engaged in a fight to the death, when Sayers finishes Steele off by cracking him over the head with the radio. While Steele is out cold, they bundle him into the bathtub and tie him up tightly with belts and rags, anything they can lay their hands on.

21 March 1947, United States Having squeezed $400 million out of the budget for the fight against "outside pressures" in Europe, Truman asked for a further $25 million to be spent on loyalty checks for all members of the FBI. During the preceding eight years, 1,429 people had been dismissed from the FBI for "treason, sedition, sabotage, espionage and a variety of radicalisms." But according to A. Devitt Vanech of the FBI, even such widespread sackings had not dealt with the problem and the remaining subversives "must all be pruned at once".

When Steele regains consciousness, Loengard quizzes him about the Hive's plans for the Sullivan theatre. Steele refuses to disclose anything. Frustrated, Loengard calls the Attorney General's office to let him know that they've got a Hiver. The Attorney General makes arrangements for another secret rendezvous, but when Loengard arrives at the abandoned warehouse for the meeting, he discovers that Majestic have tracked him down through a phone tap. Bach quickly finds out that Loengard has Steele and Loengard promises to hand the Hiver over, if Majestic help him to unveil the truth about the advertising experiment and the Sullivan show.

Bach despatches a group of his men to the headquarters of Synduct Research immediately. Hargrove and Burnside are packing their experimental equipment away when Majestic burst in on them. Burnside manages to slip away but Hargrove is shot three times. Albano has her head wrapped in a Ganglion Containment device.

Examining the experimental film, Loengard and Bach find the Hive blips, including one which says simply "Money, money," a phrase from the song that made Sayers try to jump out of a moving cab. Dr. Halligan agrees that the evidence seems to suggest hypnotic suggestion. When this is added to Bach's news that Christopher Weatherly and his son were indeed both victims of abduction, it seems clear that the Hive has been trying to persuade throwbacks to self-destruct. The

"Money, money" trigger leads them back to The Beatles, since this could be one of the songs The Beatles sing when the Ed Sullivan show goes out to 70 million people. However, since Halligan is certain that subliminal programming is only good for 36 hours, there is a chance that postponing the Beatles show could ruin the Hive's plan.

Loengard heads for the Sullivan theatre again, this time with Majestic in tow. All the commercial breaks planned for the show are checked for spliced-in frames but they reveal nothing suspicious. Bach decides that there is no need to stop the show but Loengard is not convinced. He talks to a BBC technician, Kenneth Parkinson, who tells Loengard that he was attacked while investigating an odd cable leading from his equipment. Meanwhile, Sayers spots Christopher Weatherly Snr. who is working at the theatre as a janitor. When Weatherly attacks Loengard, the Hive's involvement is all but confirmed.

Sayers has worked out that the Hive must be trying to drop images into the program via the mystery cable. Loengard follows the cable via the air conditioning chutes until he finds its origin and discovers that Burnside is wiring the cable up. Burnside spots Loengard and a fight ensues, during which the Hiver is electrocuted by his own equipment.

With the Hive cable detached from the rest of the broadcasting equipment, the Ed Sullivan Show goes ahead. All seems to be progressing well until Sayers spots Marnie Lane in the audience. Unlike the excited fans around her, she is staring straight ahead and suddenly starts to walk towards the edge of the theatre's upper circle, with the intention of hurling herself to her death. Fortunately, Loengard manages to pull her back from the brink and they watch the rest of the show from the safety of the edge of the stage.

Tipped off by Sayers and Loengard, Majestic go to collect Steele from the bath where he has been left bound and gagged. When they get there however, they discover nothing but an empty bath and a couple of bloody rags. Steele is on the run again.

See:

Abduction Experiences – Ganglion Containment Device
Steele – The Beatles – Grays – Synduct Research
Blipverts – Hargrove, Donna – Weatherly, Jr.
Burnside, Ron – Lane, Marnie – Weatherly, Snr.
Epstein, Brian – Parkinson, Kenneth

EPISODE FIVE
Dreamland

WRITER
Steve Aspis

DIRECTOR
Winrich Kolbe

GUEST STARS
Joey Aresco
Jack Conley
Louan Gideon
Andrew Hawkes
Scott Jaeck
Tim Kelleher
Tyler Layton
Madison Mason

CO-STARRING
Cashier : Gary Carter
Lieutenant : Paul Terrell Clayton
Doorman : Mark McPherson

Las Vegas, April 10, 1964. Upstairs in a large dark room overlooking the Strip, a mystery man watches the action downstairs in the glittering casino of the Desert Inn on a console of TV monitors. At a blackjack table, a young man named George is on a winning streak, observed by Jack Gettings, a casino floor manager.

When George gets up to cash in his winnings he is pursued by Susan Swenson, a cocktail waitress. Susan had been sent to persuade George to part with some of his hard-earned cash in the hospitality suite. But before Susan can do her bit to help casino cashflow, they are interrupted by a man named Cochran. He is looking for George. More specifically, he is looking for the money George has just won. When George hesitates to hand the money over, Cochran mysteriously suggests that "George Dover needs strengthening. We need him to meet Dreamland" before opening his mouth to reveal a ganglion tendril. The tendril slithers from Cochran's mouth to George's throat. Susan is terrified when Cochran then steps into the room to find her. But he doesn't hurt her. He merely picks up a wad of cash that George has forgotten and gives Susan one hundred dollars "for her trouble."

The next time we see George the high roller, he is driving a dirt hauler at the front of a convoy crossing the desert on Highway 95. The convoy passes Sayers and Loengard who have broken down in the desert. Loengard thinks that they may just about be able to make it to Las Vegas. They are running out of money too but think that if they go to Las Vegas they may be able to cash in some of the Desert Inn gambling chips they found in Agent Steele's possession. Sayers is also toying with the idea of trying to get some work.

Back at the Desert Inn, Susan recounts the story of her Hive encounter to the mystery man in the TV control room. He is most interested by the fact that they mentioned "Dreamland" but dismisses the ganglion exchange as a figment of Susan's drunken imagination.

When Sayers and Loengard arrive in Vegas later that day, they do indeed cash in some of Steele's chips. Sayers also inquires about a job and is told to talk to Mr. Gettings. The cashier seems friendly enough but as soon as Sayers and Loengard have left his desk, the cashier calls the Mystery Man upstairs to let him know that "we have two more". When we next see Sayers, on the mystery man's screens, she is dressed as a cocktail waitress, on her first shift delivering drinks to thirsty gamblers.

Taking drinks to a couple on the $100 blackjack table, Sayers suddenly experiences a peculiar buzzing sensation. When she looks around, she makes eye contact with Cochran, the man Susan saw with the ganglion in his mouth. Sayers wanders across to Loengard, who is waiting for her to come off her shift, and describes the buzzing to him. He puts it down to the noise and tiredness, but Sayers is not convinced. After all, it only happens when she goes near the $100 blackjack table, where a middle-aged couple are winning big. Suddenly it occurs to Loengard that Steele's chips were all from the $100 blackjack table. Perhaps this buzzing sensation has something to do with the Hive.

While Sayers and Loengard discuss the possibility that they have stumbled upon some Hivers, Gettings, the floor manager, interrupts them to offer them a suite in the casino where they can stay until they have settled in Vegas. Too short of cash to argue, they accept his hospitality. Sayers continues with her work, while Loengard decides to follow the winners from the $100 table when they leave the casino. Out in the car park, he sees them loading their winnings into a car, with no semblance of celebration of their luck, before they drive off into the night with the mysterious Mr. Cochran.

Loengard describes the unemotional winners to Sayers as they settle into the hospitality suite that night, unaware that they are being surveilled by the man upstairs. Sayers is disturbed by the thought that she may be picking up the telepathic frequency of the Hive but when she panics that the ganglion might be growing back, Loengard reassures her that Dr. Hertzog's experiments have shown that while some ganglion tendrils may remain in Kim's brain, they can never regenerate. Reassured by this, Sayers comes to think that perhaps she could use this "Buzz" to track Hivers down.

PLANET EARTH TIMELINE

Inexplicable

24 and 29 June 1947, Oregon, United States Pilot Kenneth Arnold encountered twenty-five small brass-coloured objects over La Grande Valley Oregon. His claim was investigated by Special Agent Frank M. Brown of the FBI who reported that "It is the personal opinion of the interviewer that Arnold actually saw what he states he saw." A newspaper report of the incident coined the expression "flying saucer".

Suddenly, four men burst into the hospitality suite and Loengard and Sayers are taken out into the hall. Thinking they might have been captured by Majestic or the Hive, they are surprised when they are asked to shower and taken to see the mystery man upstairs. In the safety of his room, lit only by flickering TV screens, the mystery man introduces himself as eccentric billionaire Howard Hughes.

Cleanliness-obsessed Hughes explains to them that they had to be showered to rid them of any dangerous bacteria. Then he hands Loengard his Majestic ID and explains that he had them investigated after they cashed a marked chip. When Hughes then talks of "them" counting cards and communicating telepathically to rob the casino, Sayers and Loengard start to think that Hughes knows about the Hive, particularly when he refers to "their common cause" which is "World domination". However, he then goes into a rant about communism and Loengard realises that Hughes has mistaken the Hive for a bunch of altogether less harmful communist agents.

Loengard wants to get away from Hughes but Sayers decides that they can turn Hughes' hatred of the communists to their advantage anyway, since they both want to keep tabs on the same group of people whoever they really are. Hughes provides Sayers and Loengard with a fantastic car, a red Mustang convertible, which they use to track the next group of big winners out into the desert. The suspected-Hivers suddenly turn off the main road into a quarry. By the time Sayers and Loengard have turned into the quarry too, the Hivers' car has disappeared.

After this dead end, Sayers decides that she wants to go along with Hughes' plan to infiltrate the Hivers at the gaming tables. Hughes arranges for a game to be fixed so that Sayers can win. He gives Sayers a small transmitter, hidden in a bag, and promises that he will have three cars on the Hivers' tail if she leaves the casino with them.

Inexplicable

July 1947, Idaho, United States Captain Ed. J Smith and Ralph Stevens were flying a DC-3 over Emmet, Idaho, when they encountered five unidentified objects, one large and four smaller objects which seemed to be under the large one's control. They estimated that the largest of the objects was easily as big as their own craft before the UFOs disappeared with a burst of incredible speed.

Sayers joins "Tammy" and "Fred" at the $100 blackjack table. When they make eye contact with her, she experiences the Buzz. Loengard watches from a distance, joined by Susan, the waitress. Susan starts to waffle about Dreamland and tells Loengard that whoever the people on the blackjack table are, they definitely aren't communists.

Meanwhile, Sayers is winning easily. As are Tammy and Fred. Suddenly, Tammy announces that it is time to leave and Sayers follows them out to their car. When Loengard realises what is happening, he tries to follow too. Outside the casino he encounters Hughes, who is waiting to pursue the Hivers, his communists, in a black Lincoln. But first Loengard wants to know about "Dreamland", or he threatens to pull Sayers out of the whole set-up. Hughes obliges willingly. "Dreamland" is the code name of Area 51. An ultra-top-security aircraft test site, situated fifty miles north of the quarry where Loengard and

Sayers lost the Hiver car. Hughes thinks that the "communists" are trying to dig their war into Dreamland.

Loengard wants to call the Pentagon but Hughes wants to be the one to foil the communists' plan himself. Realising that Hughes is totally mad, Loengard tries to get Sayers out of trouble but instead finds himself marched back into the casino at gunpoint by Gettings.

Inside the car it is already too late for Sayers when she discovers that one of her fellow passengers is Agent Steele. Unable to get out, Sayers is forced to go with Steele to the quarry, with Hughes and his men in pursuit. Fortunately, things are looking up for Loengard, who is rescued from Gettings' custody by Susan who threatens her former boss with a gun. Susan loses her job, of course, but Loengard gets to call Washington.

Meanwhile at the quarry, Sayers panics as the Hive driver puts his foot down and heads straight for the quarry wall. When she can bear to open her eyes again, she discovers that they haven't crashed. Instead they are right inside the rock, where a lot of industrious activity is centred around a huge shaft leading to who knows where. On the other side of the wall, Hughes and his men stand bewildered, confused as to where the car they were pursuing could have gone. They track the bleeping of Sayers' radio transmitter, only to discover that it has been abandoned on their side of the wall.

Inside the Hive's hidden headquarters, Steele leads Sayers into a construction trailer, where she is strapped into a chair to await her fate. Steele reaches for a jar containing a number of wriggling, snapping creatures. They look like some kind of worm, but no worm Sayers has seen on this earth. Steele picks one of the creatures out of the jar, holding it carefully in a pair of tongs. It is a buzzworm, the ganglion's natural predator. He lays a couple of the worms on Sayers' chest, promising her that they'll find their own way in.

PLANET EARTH
TIMELINE
Dark Skies

2 July 1947, Roswell, New Mexico
Captain Frank Bach was among assembled military staff at Roswell Air Force Base on the night of the Roswell incident. Bach masterminded the attack on the alien craft which led President Truman to put him in charge of all alien intelligence operations from that moment on. (The Awakening)

Hughes and his men are still trying to find a way through the quarry wall when a dirt hauler arrives, driven by George Dover. George drives like a madman, heading straight for the wall, but before he can drive on through, Hughes' men take him out with their guns. The truck comes to a halt. Hughes opens the door of the truck to examine its driver. He is dead, but something seems to be coming out of his mouth. Before Hughes can get away, a ganglion tendril lands on his face and makes an attempt to enter Hughes' body. Loengard warns him to keep his mouth shut and Hughes manages to pull it off his face so that Loengard can kill the creature. But Hughes' ordeal sends him into hysterics, giving Loengard a chance to take over.

Loengard hauls George Dover out of his truck and climbs into his place. Backing the truck up, Loengard prepares to drive straight through the wall. As he speeds towards it, uttering a suicidal scream, the truck miraculously disappears just at that moment when it should be squashed to pieces and Loengard finds himself unhurt on the other side.

Loengard arrives just in time to save Sayers. Still in his truck, he drives straight at Steele, sending him flying. Loengard heads for the trailer where Sayers is being held and pulls the buzzworms off her. He manages to free her hands before they are found by Cochran. Loengard is out of ammunition and it seems that all might be lost when Sayers takes the initiative and showers Cochran with the buzzworms still remaining in Steele's jar. Cochran screams in pain as the buzzworms take hold, leaving Sayers and Loengard free to make a run for it.

They run in the only direction they can, towards the mystery tunnel. They don't know where it will lead to, but it's their only hope . . . Until a pair of lights shines out from inside and they discover that the only exit has been blocked off.

Slowly, the lights emerge from the tunnel and Loengard and Sayers collapse with relief when out of the tunnel comes, not more Hivers, but an Air Force Jeep carrying armed police. The Hivers scuttle away like cockroaches.

Howard Hughes' brief encounter with the ganglion has turned a mild eccentric into a total obsessive. Susan the waitress has decided that Vegas is no longer her "Dreamland" and she heads for Des Moines to start a new life. No longer working for Hughes, Sayers and Loengard have to give up the fancy car that went with the job but their own vehicle has been mended and at last they too can leave town. They drink champagne in the desert outside the high wire fence of the infamous Area 51. In the darkening sky above them, they see a shooting star. Or is it?

MUSIC
Danke Schoen by Wayne Newton

See:
Alma – Domino Theory – Steele – Area 51
Dover, George – Swenson, Susan – Buzz – Dreamland
The Lady Dies Young – Buzzworms – Gettings, Jack
USSR – Cochran – Hughes, Howard – Communism
Rawlings – Containment – Ricky

EPISODE SIX
Inhuman Nature

WRITER
Melissa Rosenberg

DIRECTOR
Rodman Flender

GUEST STARS
John Dennis Johnston

James F Kelley

Charley Lang

Deborah May

Conor O'Farrell

Maury Sterling

CO-STARRING

Oldest Boehm Son	:	Zach Hopkins
Activist	:	Jeff Juday
Marian Boehm	:	Suzanne Anderson Kennedy
Youngest Boehm Son	:	Seth Murray
Jennifer Bach	:	Vanessa Munday
Mrs. Bach	:	Nancy Stephens
Middle Boehm Daughter	:	Lauren Zabel

It is April 11th 1964. Just outside Monticello, Wisconsin, a farmer and his wife are disturbed by the sound of their cattle lowing unhappily in the fields behind their house. When Farmer Boehm goes to investigate the trouble, he finds his cattle stampeding away from a number of shadowy figures who are surrounding the body of one collapsed cow. Boehm raises his gun, but before he can shoot, he is shocked from his aim by a beam of brilliant white light. Boehm watches in amazement as the shadowy figures are sucked up by the beam. The cow they leave behind is dead, her body badly mutilated and burned.

On a rare visit home, Captain Bach is reading the story of Tom Thumb to his daughter when he hears about the incident at Boehm's farm. Meanwhile Loengard and Sayers are already

on their way to Monticello to meet the Attorney General, Bobby Kennedy, who has arranged another rendezvous in the middle of nowhere. When Loengard and Sayers meet with Kennedy, he brings them the bad news that for the time being Majestic is untouchable, due to the Executive Order which protects it. If a new Executive Order were to be signed, things could be different. Loengard takes this to mean that Kennedy is planning to talk to President Johnson, but Kennedy actually wants to wait until he is President himself. Only problem is, Kennedy couldn't possibly be President until 1968, four years away.

Loengard and Sayers try to hide their disappointment as Kennedy gives them money to continue their quest and a gun to protect themselves before he returns to Washington to make a statement on the Pope and the birth control Pill. Loengard and Sayers head on to the Boehm farm. During the drive there, Sayers pulls out her own packet of birth control pills and takes one, disappointed by the knowledge that she may have to wait another four years before she and Loengard can start thinking about having a family.

At the Boehm farm they find the Boehm children milking an unhappy looking cow called Lily. When Loengard examines Lily he finds three triangular shaped marks on her left flank but before he can make a close examination of the marks, which also form a perfect triangle in relation to each other, Farmer Boehm himself bursts in upon them, armed with a gun. He suspects the strangers of being from the Department of Agriculture and only starts to open up to them when Sayers insists on telling him the truth about their visit.

2 July 1947, Roswell, New Mexico, United States
An unidentified flying object was forced out of the sky by what appeared to be a bolt of lightning but may have been anti-aircraft fire. The resulting wreckage was taken to Roswell Air Base in New Mexico, who subsequently released a number of conflicting press releases regarding what had been found. The first press release, authorised by Colonel William Blanchard, claimed that a flying saucer had been recovered. Days later came a press release stating that the wreckage was nothing more than a weather balloon.

Meanwhile, the mutilated cow has found its way to a University of Wisconsin laboratory as the subject of a necropsy performed by trainee vet Mark Waring. On close inspection, it appears that the cow has been eviscerated with amazing surgical precision and subjected to high intensity heat. The cow's abdominal cavity is strangely devoid of haemorrhage. However, before Waring can complete his necropsy, he is interrupted by Albano and his Majestic henchmen. Albano has a warrant to confiscate the complete contents of the laboratory and a non-disclosure form for Waring to sign. As Albano does indeed have the laboratory cleared out and the cow's body confiscated, he warns Waring that any mention of the incident to the press or the public will invite criminal charges and probable imprisonment.

Sayers and Loengard travel to the university to find out more about Boehm's cow but arrive too late. When they manage to slip past the university receptionist, Mrs. Elwood, they find Mark Waring lying on his slab but no cow. Realising that Majestic must have beaten them to the lab, Loengard persuades Waring that he can trust his latest visitors with whatever evidence he has left. Fortunately Waring has retained the film of his necropsy and when the photos are developed they see that, like the cow in the milking shed, the dead cow's flank had a series of triangular punctures in its side. Loengard decides that it could be time to bring Lily the live cow in for a proper examination.

At Majestic HQ, the dead cow is the subject of another

autopsy. Majestic's own veterinary expert, Dr. Halligan, suggests that the cow died immediately and without struggle. He compares the three triangular perforations on the cow's flank to those found on previous subjects on other farms in New Mexico, Colorado and Texas.

Back at the University, Lily the cow's abdomen has become distended. Waring removes the three triangular nodules and finds that they are in fact the heads of long hollow rods, which could be used to extract something from the cow, or to feed something in.

Waring subjects Lily to an X-ray. When he examines the resulting films, he finds a large black oval shadow behind her ribcage – a shadow which proves impenetrable by X-ray. Boehm suggests that the shadow is a calf, but it is not in the cow's uterus. Instead, it seems to be in her rumen, the cow's third pre-stomach.

Suddenly, Loengard jumps back from Lily with a start. He has been using the stethoscope to listen to her heart, but when Loengard hands the stethoscope back to Waring, the trainee vet confirms the impossible. The shadowy mass in Lily's stomach has its own heartbeat. Waring diagnoses an abnormal pregnancy but decides to perform an autopsy to satisfy himself of the exact nature of the growth.

Loengard, Sayers and Boehm watch intently as Waring begins the biopsy. Eventually, he gets a hold on the growth and asks Loengard to bring the incubator table over. But Waring's triumph over removing the growth turns to fear when he sees what he has removed. The incubator now contains a sac, one and a half feet long by one foot wide. It is made of a black slippery skin-like substance and something inside it is moving.

While Waring closes the incision he has made in Lily's side, Loengard and Sayers take a coffee break outside. Apart from the strange discovery they have just made, Loengard is preoccupied with that morning's meeting with Bobby Kennedy. Sayers tries to comfort him and suggests that maybe they should wait four years anyway. It will give them a chance to get themselves into a stronger position, maybe even start a family. She knows she has given voice to Loengard's desires too, but for the moment, starting a family is unthinkable.

Back in the lab, Waring is ready to complete the evaluation by opening up the sac. As Waring prepares his scalpel, Loengard loads his gun. Waring can't understand Loengard's actions, since all he is expecting to find is a deformed calf. While Waring tries to find out exactly how much Loengard knows, their questions are answered when the creature inside the sac begins to let itself out. Everyone watches in transfixed horror as a tiny human fist punches it way through the membrane.

Boehm cannot bear to see any more and flees the laboratory. Waring gags. Loengard and Sayers just about manage to hang on as the creature finally emerges in its entirety, looking for all the world like a two year old male child.

Now they have to face the horrifying thought that the Hive are incubating human children within cows. Waring and Loengard argue over this explanation while Sayers watches the little creature in its laboratory incubator. It is still covered in slime from the sac but suddenly, Sayers opens the incubator lid and starts to wipe some of the slime away with a towel.

Loengard turns to catch Sayers laughing with the child and warns her to get away from it. Sayers refuses. Something within her tells her that the child is not yet Hive.

Farmer Boehm has not waited around to find out the truth. When Majestic arrive at his farm they find him out in his fields, systematically shooting dead every cow in his herd.

Foiled by Boehm's fear, Majestic head to the university lab, hoping to catch the last remaining cow from Boehm's herd alive. Seeing Majestic draw up outside the university, Loengard and Sayers have to make a quick decision. Sure that Majestic will kill the child just to find out what's inside, Sayers wants to flee taking the baby with her. Loengard agrees reluctantly and

Waring shows Sayers a possible escape route while Loengard stays behind to deal with Majestic when they arrive.

But Majestic are not the only people in pursuit of the baby. Sayers finds herself trapped in the service tunnel by a set of locked doors when she is joined by Mrs. Elwood, the university receptionist. Sayers hopes that Mrs. Elwood will be able to help but when the woman jumps down an entire flight of stairs and manages to land on her feet, Sayers knows that she is not exactly as she seems. Mrs. Elwood demands that Sayers hands the baby over and a fight for the child ensues, with Mrs. Elwood momentarily gaining control. However, thinking that she has knocked Sayers out, Mrs. Elwood drops her guard to unlock the door and is taken by surprise when Sayers cracks a fire extinguisher over her head. With the child back in her arms, Sayers makes a run for it once more.

In the tunnels beneath the university, Sayers is finally joined by Loengard and together they manage to give Majestic the slip. Safely outside, Loengard and Sayers drive out into the countryside with the child and ponder their next move. The child needs a home and Sayers is keen to provide that home for the child until somewhere permanent can be found. Their worrying is needless however, since, while they sleep in their Buick that night, the child is woken by a bright white light. The door to the car is mysteriously opened and the child steps out. Sayers wakes just in time to see the child ascending to a Hive ship but is unable to do anything to save him, since she and Loengard seem to have been locked inside the car.

Next day, Loengard and Sayers resume their journey alone. Captain Bach returns home from this disturbing mission, grateful for his own normal family, and reads the story of Tom Thumb to his daughter once again.

Inhuman Nature, says Megan Ward, "shows that they have become somewhat accustomed to the odd and the strange . . . I think it is in Sayers' character to believe the child is not alien and look for its purity. It's indicative of their compassion. They want to save the world one person at a time."

See:
Albano - Kaufman - Bach, Jennifer - Lily - Boehm, Kester - Waring, Mark - Boehm, Marian - Elwood, Mrs.

Ancient Future

WRITERS
James D Parriott & Gay Walch

DIRECTOR
Lou Antonio

GUEST STARS
Charley Lang
Conor O'Farrell
Eric Steinberg
Sam Vlahos
Steven Ford
Daba Gladstone
Joseph Whipp

CO-STARRING

Hiver	:	Robert Arce
Anchorman	:	Don Clark
Mission Control	:	Dan Erickson
Safe-suit man	:	Roger Hewlett
Tlingit Chief	:	Dale Ishimoto
Traveller	:	Matt Roe

Alaska, 100BC. A group of early native Alaskans, the Tlingit, are gathered around a fire while an Elder sings and makes an offering of a salmon to their gods. Suddenly, there is a bright flash that draws their attention away from the fire and to the sky. At first they think they are seeing a shooting star, but the blazing light is falling towards them, emitting some kind of vibration as it falls. It screams overhead, narrowly missing the encampment but shaking the earth with the force of a quake as it comes to land nearby.

Two thousand years later, a modern-day Tlingit, Tug Barrow, is woken from his sleep by a vibration. Unable to sleep through what might be a small quake, Tug gets up and drives out to the mountain where his Tlingit ancestors saw the falling star all those years ago. When he gets there, Tug hikes up to a rocky clearing, a special place for the Tlingit, and once again experiences some kind of vibration. Curiosity turns to fear however when Tug sees the rocks which are being shaken around him suddenly lift into the air and float as if being held there by some unseen force.

Majestic are already investigating the phenomenon of the floating rocks, putting the curious levitation down to magnetic disturbances which seem to be emanating from a fault line above the town of Chiliwack, Alaska. Loengard and Sayers are in the Alaskan town, attending a Good Friday service given by the Reverend Gary Barrow, a man with some Tlingit blood. After the service, Loengard and Sayers corner Reverend Barrow and ask if they can talk to him about his uncle Tug, the man who saw the floating rocks. Reverend Barrow is suspicious. He has had enough of journalists, but using the aliases "Kim Smith and John Lomiller", Loengard and Sayers convince him that they are students on a graduate anthropology programme and he agrees to let them meet Tug.

Tug tells them that he is the last "Tlingit-ixt", or shaman, of his clan. As a shaman he is a story-teller and he keeps the Tlingit legends alive. Now he tells the story of the star that fell out of the sky. The Tlingit were originally a nomadic people but they settled in Chiliwack when the star came to obey the wishes of the "Father who rode down on its tail". Tug explains that the "Father" spoke to the Tlingit without words, begging them to make sure that the star stayed buried within the chasm into which it had fallen "until it sang its song." If the star was taken out of the chasm before that song was heard, it would mean the end of the Tlingit. A day of massive destruction.

Sayers and Loengard listen to the legend of the star intently. Could it be that the star was in fact a crippled spacecraft and the "father" its pilot Gray? Their suspicions are confirmed

PLANET EARTH TIMELINE
On The Record

19 July 1947
Rear-Admiral Roscoe Hillenkoetter issued an unauthenticated memorandum in which he states that "The recovery of unidentified planform aircraft in the state of New Mexico on 6th July 1947... is confirmed... the craft and wreckage are not of US manufacture."

26 July 1947, United States
President Truman passed the National Security Act, which united the armed services under one control. James V. Forrestal became the first Secretary of Defence.

PLANET EARTH TIMELINE
Inexplicable

August 1947, United States
Majestic-12 - also known as Majic-12 and MJ-12 - was established by special classified executive order of President Truman.

when Tug shows them the totem pole which stands outside his
cabin. Carved by his ancestor, between the faces of bears,
eagles and fish, is the face of an alien Gray.

Loengard and Sayers persuade Tug to take them to the
mountain where the star fell. On the way up to the chasm,
Sayers tries to make sense of the concept that it was a friendly
Gray which encountered the Tlingit. Loengard tells her about
the Gray at Roswell, and the ganglion which was found
embedded in its nervous system in the same way as ganglions
have been found in human hosts. It is possible therefore that
the ganglions are in fact the Hive and that the Grays were a
benevolent race before they were taken over in the way that the
human race is being taken over now.

As they near the site of the dancing rocks, a helicopter

passes overhead. Tug explains that Air Force choppers from the Elmendorf base have been surveying the site since he first saw the rocks and when they reach the spot, it has already been surrounded by a chain-link fence. As they watch, the chopper seems to falter in the air. When this information is interpreted at Majestic, the boffins from Area 51 send news to Bach and his second Albano that "They think we've got one."

PLANET EARTH TIMELINE
On The Record

2 September 1947, Brazil
In Rio de Janeiro, the United States and 19 Latin American Nations signed the Inter-American Treaty of Reciprocal Assistance. The treaty stipulated that "an armed attack by any state shall be considered as an attack against all American States".

Back in the mountains, Loengard and Sayers are examining the rocks which once floated when the birds suddenly fall silent and the rocks do indeed begin to float. Then as suddenly as they lifted into the air, the rocks drop back to the earth. The spectacle of the floating rocks is over but before the astonished witnesses can gather themselves, they are thrown to the ground by a massive earthquake.

Bach hears of the earthquake on network news. When he discovers that its epicentre was in Chiliwack, he orders an immediate investigation while the television reports that the epicentre was Whittier on the Prince William Sound in a deliberate piece of Majestic disinformation to keep unwanted visitors away from the Chiliwack site.

Recovering from the shock of the quake, Loengard and Sayers join Reverend Barrow and Tug at the edge of a deep chasm which has suddenly appeared. From where they are standing, they cannot see the bottom of the chasm, but they can see an eerie glow. Loengard insists that they head back to Chiliwack and fetch climbing equipment.

PLANET EARTH TIMELINE
Inexplicable

12 September 1947, above the Pacific Ocean
Crew on the flight-deck of a Pan-American Airlines flight to Honolulu reported an encounter with an object emitting blue-white light which changed to reddish twin glows upon withdrawal.

Chiliwack Episcopal Church has already become a first aid centre for victims of the quake. Sayers helps to tend the victims while Loengard gathers together the equipment they need. Tug has started to sense that Loengard is not what he seems and tells him that he has the "look of a hunter who's found his prey".

Accompanied once more by Tug and Reverend Barrow, Loengard and Sayers head for the chasm under cover of darkness. Loengard is the first to go down. At the bottom of the chasm, they find the source of the glow but before they can investigate closely, they hear an odd groaning sound and are suddenly wracked by some kind of magnetic force. Only Loengard seems relatively unaffected.

Meanwhile, Bach, who is preparing his own assault on the chasm, has received news that Loengard has beaten him to it and ups the pace of the Majestic mission.

In the chasm, Loengard and Sayers finally see the alien ship. Strange glyphs are the only definable features on the metallic arc that perhaps only represents a tenth of the ship's total mass. Loengard explains to Barrow and Tug that this is not a miracle but a spacecraft. It is larger than the craft found at Roswell and when Loengard goes to touch it, he discovers that it is giving off heat yet the surface of the craft is not hot.

Once again, the ship begins to emit a hum and all but Loengard have to leave the chasm for fear of being taken ill. Loengard remains to take photographs of the ship and as he is doing so he recognises one of the glyphs. It is the one that Sayers drew on the map, the one that Loengard saw in the wheatfield. Loengard touches the surface of the ship and is suddenly overtaken by a vision of the future. He sees himself having an argument with Bach, begging him to leave the ship in its place. He sees the ship being lifted from the fissure in a cradle winched by a helicopter. He sees the ship explode in mid-air. Next, Loengard sees himself as an old man, crawling along parched earth surrounded by the bones of long dead men. When he asks his companion who these people were, the man tells him that the corpses were throwbacks. The only people remaining on earth are throwbacks now. As the elderly Loengard collapses and gives up hope, a huge triangular ship, like the Black Knight seen by the astronaut on the Gemini mission, passes quickly overhead. The Hive has won.

Though Bach has been having trouble trying to persuade General Thompson that Chiliwack should be isolated, the Majestic agents arrive at the chasm in time to pull Loengard out before he comes to too much harm. By now he is delirious and they take him to the church to recover. When he comes round however, he remembers his vision and knows that it is important. Summoned to meet Bach, Loengard uses the opportunity to warn Bach against removing the ship from the fissure and finds himself having the very conversation he saw in his vision. Bach is unconvinced and sneers at Loengard. He was, after all, delirious when Bach's men pulled him out of the chasm. Bach commands his men to go ahead with the plan to airlift the spaceship out of its resting place.

Back in the church, Tug and his nephew are praying side by side despite their differing spiritual views. Sayers and Loengard use the peace to discuss their next move before Sayers helps Loengard to hi-jack the officers guarding them by distracting the men by asking "What's a girl gotta do to get a cup of coffee around here?" With the guards as hostages, Loengard and Sayers hi-jack a helicopter and fly out to confront Colonel Bach who is already having the ship hooked up to the lifting gear on his own helicopter.

The magnetic pulses given off by the ship are getting shorter and coming more quickly. Sayers realises that if the pulses get much faster they will join together in one continuous tone. Perhaps this could be the song of which the ancient father spoke.

While Loengard tries to reason with Bach, he orders his pilot to hover directly in front of Bach's helicopter to prevent him from being able to pull the ship out of the chasm. Eventually Loengard manages to persuade Bach that if he is wrong about the prophecy, then waiting a little while longer to pull the ship out will not make a real difference. Bach gives in to Loengard's demands and orders that the mission be abandoned for the time being. Just as the site is evacuated, the magnetic pulses

finally join together in one long tone and the ship explodes in the fissure, just as the ancient Tlingit legend predicted.

Loengard and Sayers give thanks for their lives at the Easter Sunday service in Reverend Barrow's church. Even Bach is there to give praise. He stands alone at the back of the congregation. An enlightened man.

February 1948, United States Brigadier General C.P.Cabell, chief of the Air Intelligence Requirements Division, requested that every military base in America be equipped with an interceptor-type aircraft.

See:
Barrow, Rev. Gary — Barrow, Tug
Mittermeyer, Ernst — Tlingit

Hostile Convergence

WRITER
Javier Grillo-Marxuach

DIRECTOR
Perry Lang

GUEST STARS
Robert Carradine
Charley Lang
Diane Cary
Jack Lindine
Jamie Denton
Conor O'Farrell
Stephanie Faracy
Lisa Waltz
Richard Gilliland
Sam Whipple
Tim Kelleher

CO-STARRING

Mayor Holm Bursum	:	Conrad Bachman
Joe Edermeyer	:	David Brisbin
Clark Balfour	:	Terence Evans
Allen Dulles	:	Mike Kennedy
Kate Balfour	:	Wendy Robie

Socorro, New Mexico. April 24, 1964. Police officer Lonnie Zamora fills his coffee-flask in a roadside diner before going on duty. Later that night, he gets involved in a high speed car chase which ends abruptly when the car in front is suddenly obscured by a bright flash of light accompanied by a deafening roar. Suspecting that an old dynamite shack might have blown up, Zamora follows the direction of the flashes to a valley, but finds no dynamite shack. Instead, about eight hundred feet away, he sees a shiny silver object shimmering in the last of the sun. It is saucer-shaped and rests on short, squat legs. Shocked by what he is seeing, Zamora stumbles back

against his car and when he next looks up, the saucer is taking off at high speed into the sky above him.

Later the next day, Sayers and Loengard are on their way to Socorro to investigate Officer Zamora's claims. When they break their journey near Kansas, Sayers calls home and is greeted with the news that her elder sister, Andrea, is about to get married. Back in the car, Sayers begs to be allowed to go back to Denver for the wedding but Loengard is adamant that they should investigate the Socorro sighting first.

5 April 1948, New Mexico, United States
Three trained balloon observers reported a sighting of a UFO in the vicinity of Hollman Air Force Base, New Mexico. The UFO allegedly executed a number of violent manoeuvres at high speed before disappearing suddenly.

30 April 1948, United States
Lieutenant Commander Marcus Lowe witnessed a light coloured sphere in the sky to the south of Anacostia Naval Air Station.

Majestic already know all about Loengard and Sayers' "little domestic tiff", when Bach joins Allen Dulles to watch the screening of a 16 mm film. The subject of the film is Jack Ruby, the man who shot Lee Harvey Oswald. He is pacing his cell, ranting and raving. Bach wants to be allowed to talk to him and

Dulles wants to know if Ruby can reveal the name of the "third shooter" of JFK's assassination but neither Bach nor Dulles can have Ruby until the Warren Commission has seen him.

While Bach and Dulles discuss the possibility of getting Ruby out of Dallas, Ruby has a visitor. Dressed in the clothes of a jail worker, ex-Majestic agent Steele is taking Ruby his lunch. Ruby begs Steele to "Strengthen" him but Steele just tells Ruby to eat his lunch instead. Steele slides the food tray under the door and leaves Ruby alone again. The lunch looks innocent enough until Ruby bites into a hot-dog. Before he knows what is happening, Ruby has a buzzworm in his mouth. The ganglions' only natural predator, the buzzworm has been planted by Steele to scavenge the remaining ganglion tendrils in Ruby's system, thus rendering him harmless to the Hive and useless to Majestic.

Sayers and Loengard finally reach Socorro, which is already buzzing with reporters and UFO fans. They decide to stop for lunch in the diner where Zamora bought his coffee on that fateful night. While Loengard and Sayers wait for "Flyin' Saucer Special" (split pea soup with ham), the waitress, Cassie, passes Loengard a napkin onto which have been written the words "Dark Skies". Loengard recognises it as the password he used with Jesse Marcel in Dallas and sure enough, Marcel is in the diner too. Loengard joins Marcel when he goes to listen to the story of Officer Zamora. Sayers stays in the diner, eating her soup, and finds herself in a conversation with Cassie. Sayers explains the predicament of her sister's wedding and Cassie advises her that if she still wants to make it to Denver in time, Sayers can catch a bus which will be passing by the diner in twenty minutes' time.

Unaware that Sayers is about to split, Loengard listens intently to Zamora's story. Zamora describes the craft he saw as being "egg-shaped, sitting there on the ground like it was Easter Sunday." Somehow this does not seem quite right to

PLANET EARTH TIMELINE

Inexplicable

15 June 1948, Montana, United States
Mr. Booneville of Miles City, Montana, reported the appearance of an object that had a reddish glow and a tail, which was moving at twice the speed of any conventional aircraft.

16 June 1948, USSR
Soviet Air Force pilot Arkadii Ivanovich Apraskin encountered a craft shaped like a cucumber, which radiated light beams towards the ground. His sighting was confirmed by radar at the airbase of Kapustin Yar. Staff there reported that the craft had disobeyed orders to land.

1 July 1948, United States
Major Hammer of the Rapid City Air Base reported the appearance of 12 discs near said base. The discs were 100 feet in diameter and travelling at 500 miles per hour before they disappeared without warning.

Loengard. Neither does Zamora's description of the "men" who emerged from the egg, dressed in white overalls. Marcel too is confused. He tells Loengard that Zamora's description does not fit in with what he, Marcel, saw at Roswell either. Marcel then asks Loengard whether he has heard of Area 51. When it is obvious that Loengard has heard about the top-secret defence base, Marcel invites him to meet someone who worked there for many years. Marcel's former colleague Clark Balfour is now dying of cancer in the town of Magdalena, twenty miles from Socorro.

Of course Loengard has to follow this lead up, but when he goes to find Kim, he discovers that she has taken the bus to Denver, leaving him his soup and a note. Her note tells him that "Living our lives can be as important as defending them . . . It's hard to put up a good fight without experiencing a little of what you're fighting for."

Meanwhile, in the diner, the kindly waitress Cassie makes a call. She tells the person at the other end "She's going to Denver." Agent Steele replies "Qua-fu Denver Kek-ba."

17 July 1948, New Mexico, United States
Staff at Kirkland Air Force Base, New Mexico described a sighting in the vicinity of San Acacia. The UFOs were travelling in excess of 1,500 miles per hour in a "J" formation at an altitude of 20,000 ft. Later, their formation was seen to alter to the shape of a circle.

20 July 1948, Arnhem, the Netherlands
Mr. A.D. Otter, chief investigator of the Court of Damage Inquiry, and his young daughter, witnessed the passing of a wingless aircraft with two decks passing at an unusually high speed and altitude.

25 July 1948, United States
Captain Clarence S Chiles and his co-pilot were alarmed by a UFO on a collision course with their DC-3. The craft coming towards them appeared to be 100 feet long, shaped like a cigar, but without any wings or rudder. As it approached, the craft gave off an intense dark blue glow.

Loengard and Marcel head on to visit Balfour. In his bed at the Magdalena Hospital, Balfour is almost dead. When he can bring himself to speak, Balfour confirms Loengard's suspicions that the Socorro sighting was "not alien". He then tells them with his dying breath that he has the plans of the ship Zamora saw. His wife, Kate, hands Marcel an envelope containing keys. On the outside of the envelope is a drawing of the symbol that Zamora claimed to have seen on the side of the ship. Inside are instructions as to where the plans can be found.

In the Dallas cellblock where Jack Ruby is being held, Albano lets Bach know that Loengard and Marcel have met with Balfour and taken the keys. Bach then turns his attention to Ruby, who has been put under sedation. While Bach inspects the remains of Ruby's lunch, Ruby suddenly ejects the buzzworm, considerably fatter than when it first slipped down his throat.

Arriving at her family home in Denver, Sayers is fitted for her Maid of Honour dress and finds out about her sister's new fiancé. Andrea Sayers had know Rob Weller for just three weeks, during which time her mother complains that he has been "always on a plane." Andrea retorts that is because Rob "works for the government" but exactly what he does "he keeps that pretty much to himself". While the women discuss the reception, which is to be held at the house, Rob introduces himself. He seems like a very handsome, charming man.

Back at the Socorro site, Cassie from the diner comforts Loengard while Officer Zamora repeats his well-worn tale. Marcel has been examining the spot where the craft actually landed and his suspicions are aroused by the scorched earth he finds there, since as far as he can remember, the Roswell craft never had to touch down.

The crowds listening to Zamora are suddenly joined by a man Loengard recognises as J. Allen Hynek, head investigator of Project Blue Book. He calls Zamora's sighting "the most valid of the flying disc reports to date". John is disturbed by this comment which seems to admit that the disc was real. He is also bothered by the fact that Majestic are nowhere to be seen. In fact, Bach is busy at Majestic HQ, showing Dulles the buzzworm which came out of Ruby's mouth. Meanwhile, ex-Majestic man Steele has found an announcement for a very interesting society wedding in the *Denver Post*.

Marcel and Loengard decide that it is time to find out what Balfour has hidden. They find a stainless steel tube, of the type that usually contains plans, beneath the wreckage of a car. An envelope found with the tube contains a notarised affidavit, requiring that the tube be opened by key in front of witnesses. Loengard

3 August 1948, USSR
An American journalist spotted an object, similar to that seen by Captain Chiles and his co-pilot, travelling at high velocity in the skies near Moscow.

1 October 1948, North Dakota, United States
2nd Lieutenant George F Gorman was cruising at an altitude of 4,500 feet above Fargo, North Dakota, when he became aware of an intermittent white light travelling approximately 3,000 ft below him. When he tried to intercept the light, it seemed to take action to evade him.

16 February 1949, New Mexico, United States
A conference was called at the Los Alamos National Laboratory to discuss recent UFO phenomena.

and Steele decide to find those witnesses in Socorro, unaware that someone has already witnessed them finding the tube.

6 May 1949, USSR
Soviet-pilot Apraskin encountered another cucumber shaped object. This time the craft attacked, damaging Apraskin's cockpit and forcing him to make an emergency landing due to a sudden loss of air pressure.

Back in Denver, Sayers gets a chance to talk to her future brother-in-law on his own. Asking Sayers about Loengard, Rob lets slip that "Andy said you were in Kansas". This arouses Sayers' suspicion for, as far as she can remember, she never mentioned the fact to her sister. While she takes a call from Loengard, who is about to open the plan tube in front of a hungry crowd at the Socorro diner, Sayers voices her suspicions and goes through the pockets of Rob's jacket, which is draped over her chair. Finding lots of business cards she reads out the name "Swofford Towing" which Loengard recognises instantly as a Majestic field office. Suddenly, Sayers realises that Rob is not all he seems.

Sayers is caught red-handed by her sister, who is disbelieving of Sayers' explanation that Rob is a Majestic spy. However, when Andrea asks Sayers why she wants to undermine the marriage with lies, Rob suddenly appears behind them and announces that Sayers has been telling the truth after all.

Hanging up on Sayers, Loengard is also worried. He calls Magdalena hospital and discovers that they have no records of patient Clark Balfour. The realisation that Sayers is being kept under observation by Majestic in Denver and the fact that Balfour was never officially a patient at Magdalena make Loengard suspect a Majestic plot. Figuring that the "plans" which Marcel now holds may be a piece of Majestic disinformation and mean nothing, Loengard halts the opening of the tube and heads for Denver saying "Kim needs me."

Loengard is only too right. A catering van has just arrived at the Sayers' homestead, driven by none other than Jim Steele. Inside the house, Rob Weller is telling Andrea the full story of how he came to be with her. He was indeed sent by Majestic, but he assures Andrea that he hasn't changed his mind about wanting her for his wife.

While Andrea struggles to take in the things she has just learned, her sister answers the door to the catering team. Looking through the window by the door, she immediately recognises Steele and warns Rob, but before they can get Andrea and Mrs. Sayers to safety, the Hivers knock down the door and rush in. A gun-fight ensues, during which one of the Hivers and Rob are shot. Sayers and her mother manage to remain hidden, but upstairs, Andrea calls out and Steele is attracted by her voice. He starts up the stairway to find her, with Sayers in pursuit. Unknown to Sayers, as she sets her sights on Steele, another Hiver is setting his sights on her. Just as he is about to fire however, he is blown away by an unseen gunman, later revealed to be Rob, leaving Sayers free to fire at Steele. She catches him with a bullet in the shoulder but before she can finish him off, Steele escapes through an open window. Loengard doesn't arrive until darkness falls.

Back in the Socorro diner, Jesse Marcel sits pondering the plan tube with newspaper reporter Joe Edermeyer. Disillusioned, Marcel breaks open the

21 July 1949, Washington DC, United States
The United States Senate ratified NATO (the North Atlantic Treaty Organisation). This organisation committed the United States to a mutual defence alliance with 11 other countries. The treaty was actually signed in Washington DC on April 4, by Canada, Great Britain, France, Belgium, Italy, The Netherlands, Luxembourg, Norway, Sweden, Ireland and Iceland. The treaty stated that its purpose was to: "safeguard the freedom, common heritage and civilisation of their peoples founded on the principles of democracy, individual liberty and the rule of law."

tube and pulls out a set of blueprints. As soon as he sees the plans of an egg-shaped saucer with German instructions and a Nazi Swastika prominently displayed on the saucer's door, Marcel knows he has been duped. He knows that it would suit Majestic's purposes perfectly for people to think that the Nazis had space technology. He also knows that it probably isn't true.

With the drama over for another day, Bach pays a visit on Jack Ruby, who is still recovering from his ordeal at Majestic HQ. When Ruby asks Bach where he is, Bach replies:

"Wherever you want to be, Mr. Ruby. Wherever you want to be."

MUSIC
Where did our love go? by The Supremes

See:
Balfour, Clark — Hynek, J. Allen — Sayers, Joan
Balfour, Kate — Marcel, Jesse — Steele
Bursum, Mayor Holm — Roswell Incident
Weller, Rob — Cassie — Sayers, Andrea
Zamora, Lonnie — Edermeyer, Joe

We Shall Overcome

WRITER
Bryce Zabel

DIRECTOR
Oscar Costo

STARRING
Roger Aaron Brown
Wayne Tippit
Tracy Fraim
Lorraine Toussaint
Charley Lang
Mike Kennedy
Dean Norris
Sayers Robillard
Conor O'Farrell
Raphael Sbarge

CO-STARRING

William Paley	:	Art Bell
Twining	:	Arell Blanton
Agent Foote	:	Edward Edwards
Lance Taylor	:	Terence Mathews
Lionel Tillman	:	Sean A Moran
Hubert Humphrey	:	Don Moss

June 21, 1964. Night-time in rural Mississippi. A 1951 blue Ford station wagon winds through the countryside while its occupants worriedly discuss their police pursuers. They seem to have lost them. Now the occupants of the station wagon, led by Andrew Mendel, need to find a phone so they can make a call to "headquarters."

In the dank basement of a nearby church, Reverend Langston Poole and three companions are at work in some kind of hydroponic garden. They are harvesting small pod-like plants which resemble the "freeze orb" used to immobilise Sayers during her abduction. As they work, Poole and his

companions converse in the raspy tongue of the Hive.

Hanging back from the action is a white man, Clayton Lewis. He doesn't want to get involved and when Poole goes to touch him on the shoulder, Lewis is disgusted. Poole puts Lewis's reaction down to colour prejudice and lets him leave the basement, though the Hive's plans for Lewis are not complete.

Outside the church, the station-wagon carrying Mendel and his friends pulls up. Recognising the church as one of their list of churches used for voter registration, Mendel plans to go inside and use the phone. To his surprise, the door is locked and when he peers in through the window, Mendel sees a far from conventional church service taking place.

Langston Poole is stretching out his hand towards a restrained Clayton Lewis. As Mendel watches, a ball of light appears in Poole's hand and he coerces Lewis to touch it and "experience the joys of 'singularity'". Lewis refuses, but before Poole can force him to touch the light, Poole becomes aware that they are being observed and the ball disappears as quickly as it came.

Sayers and Loengard are still on the road. Stopping near Juarez, Mexico, Loengard calls home and talks to his mother. Returning to Sayers in the car, Loengard tells her that their plan of hiding out in Mexico may have to be put on hold. The message his mother gave him was that "Mark says he's not laughing anymore and you know where to find him." Loengard thinks that the Mark in question is Mark Simonson, Loengard's old boss from his days with Congressman Pratt. The last Loengard heard of Simonson was that he was heading for Mississippi to join the Civil Rights movement. "Not laughing" refers to the fact that Simonson no longer thinks that Loengard has been joking about aliens. When Sayers then shows him a newspaper headline about missing civil rights workers, Loengard knows that they have to go to Mississippi too.

A flashback to Martin Luther King's "I have a dream" speech explains that segregation is still rife in America. The Civil Rights movement is campaigning for change, starting with a voter registration programme to encourage the black community to know its rights.

Loengard and Sayers head first for Meridian, Mississippi. Arriving there, they encounter Clayton Lewis and his side-kick Arthur Dalton Rogers. Sayers experiences a strong Hive Buzz as she passes the men and this causes her to stare at Lewis, arousing his aggression. Though Lewis tells Sayers and Loengard that they should be gone, he can't shake the gaze of Langston Poole who has been watching the whole exchange.

Back at Majestic HQ, Bach has called a meeting of Majestic's board of directors. Among those present are former CIA head Allen Dulles, Minnesota Senator Hubert Humphrey, Professor Henry Kissinger and William Paley, President of CBS.

Bach needs more money. A billion dollars over five years.

1950, Palanque, Mexico
Archaeologists uncovered an ancient Mayan tomb. On one wall of the tomb they found a drawing of a man sitting inside some kind of capsule, which appeared to have a control board inside it. From the back of the capsule came a trail of flames, leading the archaeologists to believe that they had stumbled upon an early depiction of a spacecraft.

Humphrey complains that it would be impossible to skim that kind of money from the defence budget, while Kissinger wants answers about Vietnam. There follows an interesting exchange which pulls in the JFK assassination, the Bay of Pigs fiasco and the Warren Commission. Bach insists that Majestic's nose is clean

1950, Korea
The Korean War broke out when North Korea attacked the South. The South retaliated with the help of US forces led by General MacArthur.

before he is interrupted by Albano, bringing news that Loengard is probably headed for Mississippi.

Moments later, Allen Dulles announces on television that he will be travelling to Mississippi on an FBI fact-finding mission at the behest of President Lyndon Johnson. Loengard and Sayers are watching the broadcast through the window of an electrical goods store when they are approached by a black woman who surprises them by mentioning Project Blue Book.

She introduces herself as Etta Mae Tillman and hands them a slip of paper with an address written upon it before she moves away again.

At the church, trouble is in store for Langston Poole. Clayton Lewis has decided it is time to teach Poole to "pay proper respect." Along with Rogers, Lewis storms into the church and disrupts a voter registration session. In a face-to-face confrontation with Poole, Lewis refers to a "higher law" only to be told that the "Hive answers to no God." When Lewis hits Poole, the Reverend does not respond in kind but tells him "in your mind, you fight us. But in your ways, you give us strength". He is referring to Loengard's fear that the Hive will use the human prejudices as a means of disruption.

Sayers and Loengard go to the address given to them by Etta Mae. It is her home and she is giving shelter to Mark Simonson there. Simonson tells Loengard that he was with the missing civil rights workers just before they disappeared and recounts the story of what was seen in the church. Fleeing the sight, the men realised that they were being followed again. Trying to lose the police cars on their tail, the men abandoned their own car and split up to run for it. Eventually, Simonson lost the other three and found himself in a clearing, watching the landing of a Hive ship.

Next day, while Loengard and Sayers are visiting the site where Simonson pulled his car off the road, Etta Mae brings the bad news that a car has just been found in nearby Bogue Chitto swamp, and it is believed to be the car of the missing civil rights workers. Loengard and Simonson impersonate FBI officers in order to get a look at the car. It appears that the car was burned but no bodies or bullet holes were found to suggest the fate of its occupants. While Loengard is trying to convince a real FBI officer of his credentials, Bach and his Majestic agents arrive on the scene to discover that Loengard has beaten them to it.

30 July 1950,
United States
A US Army
Intelligence
report confirmed
the sighting of
discs at an altitude of 15,000 feet
above the Hanford AEC Plant.

1950, United States
Frank Scully published "Behind the
Flying Saucers". In 1953, Scully
claimed that he had obtained a statement from Edward Ruppelt, ex-head of
the Blue Book Project. Ruppelt told
him that, "confidentially, of all the
books that have been published about
flying saucers, your book was the one
that gave us the most headaches
because it was closest to the truth."

1950, New Mexico, United States
USAF Missile engineer Daniel Fry
claimed that he had taken a ride in
an oval shaped capsule that flew him
to New York and back (a round trip of
8000 miles) in less than an hour.

Meanwhile Sayers and Etta Mae turn their attention to the church. Sayers instructs Etta May to keep the Reverend Poole busy while Sayers investigates the basement. Once inside the basement, Sayers experiences a strong Buzz and finds the pod plantation. She also becomes aware that she is not alone. Clayton Lewis is chained up in a dark corner. He has obviously been implanted.

Upstairs, Etta May grows suspicious when the Reverend talks about a plan that doesn't seem to be a holy one. She is convinced that something is very wrong when the Reverend assures her that some good will come out of the civil rights workers' death rather than condemning the violence, even though it has not been confirmed that the workers are no longer alive.

Lewis later reveals that Reverend Poole is indeed the leader of the local Hive and that Poole used telepathy to tell Lewis to kill the missing men. Despite his experiences however, Lewis is still adamant that his racial prejudice is right and though he begs for Sayers' help, she is not sure she wants to give it to him.

After much soul-searching, Loengard and Sayers decide that they cannot deny Lewis their help even if he refuses to repent his racism and Loengard begins to perform the ART.

12 May 1951,
Marshall Islands
The United States
detonated the
first H bomb on
Marshall Islands.

Though he let Loengard go free at the site where the car was pulled out of the swamp, Bach is holding Simonson. He tells Simonson that he knows he was in the car with the missing civil rights workers. Bach even has a transcript of the call Loengard made from Mexico, containing

Simonson's cryptic message. Before Bach can get any further information from Simonson however, Majestic receive news that the church may be harbouring a Hive plantation. Majestic's men remove the pods and make a study of the soil before Bach gives the order for the church to be torched. J. Edgar Hoover is on his way to Mississippi to investigate the furore and Bach wants the church burned before Hoover arrives.

When the basement has been cleared by Majestic men, the Reverend Poole is led away, extolling the virtues of the alien nation's equality, telling Bach that "While you fight amongst yourselves, we assimilate. We blend in. We have no colour. We have no conflict. You deny it. But we are your every solution." Bach then orders the firing of the church, lighting the first match himself. J. Edgar Hoover arrives just in time to see the last of the bonfire.

10 September 1951, New Jersey, United States Major Ballard and Lieutenant Rogers of the Dover Air Force Base in Delaware observed a UFO over Sandy Hook, New Jersey.

At Etta Mae's house, the ART is coming to an end but just before the ganglion is ejected, Lewis uses his telepathic powers to warn them that others are coming. Other Hive implantees are already surrounding the house. Loengard and Sayers make a run for their car with Etta Mae and Lewis, stalling the implantees by letting them have the ganglion which Lewis has just ejected.

September 1951, San Francisco, United States America signed the Tripartite Security Treaty with Australia and New Zealand to counter communist expansion in South East Asia.

Next day, Loengard has a meeting with Bach outside the remains of the church. Loengard is furious that Bach could have torched a church and accuses him of not caring about the consequences. When Loengard says that he won't clear up Bach's mess because he no longer works for Majestic, Bach warns him chillingly, "you always work for us. You're alive because it's true."

Faced with that stark fact, Loengard buys Simonson's freedom by handing Clayton Lewis over to Majestic, who will make a thorough study of him as an ART survivor. In addition, Loengard tries to extract a promise that the whereabouts of the civil rights workers' bodies will be revealed. That information arrives in an anonymous tip-off shortly after Bach and Loengard bid each other goodbye.

Back in Washington, J. Edgar Hoover meets with Majestic agent Albano outside the White House, expecting Albano to hand over a full report on the Mississippi burning. Albano hands over an envelope but instead of a report, it contains a series of photographs. Hoover is visibly sickened by the envelope's contents and tells Albano that Bach is an "Anti-American Bastard, bringing Clyde into this." Albano leaves Hoover to his thoughts, knowing that from now on Majestic will have the top cop's full co-operation.

1952, Holdstone Down, Devon, England
George King claimed that he met Jesus when a UFO landed near his home.

1952, Ohio, United States
A pilot from Wright-Patterson Air Force Base claimed to have seen the arrival at the base of three bodies retrieved from a UFO crash in Arizona. When the bodies were autopsied, they were found to have colourless blood and no digestive tracts or sex organs.

In Meridian, Mississippi, the townspeople are already getting to work on rebuilding a church. Money has come in the form of an anonymous donation, but Loengard and Sayers have good reason to believe that the mystery donor may just have been Clayton Lewis.

MUSIC
Come a Little Bit Closer by Jay and The Americans
We'll Sing in the Sunshine by Gale Garnett

See:
Dalton Rogers, Arthur — Mendel, Andrew Tolson, Clyde — Gould, David — Organic Freeze Orbs Hoover, J. Edgar — Poole, Langston Luther King, Martin — Ruby, Jack — Ku Klux Klan Simonson, Mark — Lewis, Clayton — Taylor, Lance Malcolm X — Tillman, Etta Mae

EPISODE TEN
The Last Wave

WRITER
Melissa Rosenberg

DIRECTOR
Steve Beers

GUEST STARS
Brent David Fraser
Conor O'Farrell
Brittney Powell
Christopher Wiehl
Mark Bramhall
David Markel

CO-STARRING
Supervisor : Carl Garfalio
Surfer : Kristoffer Ryan Winters

July 20, 1964. Down on the beach, a group of bronzed Californian kids are having a party. The surf is up but keen surfer Dewey has more on his mind than waves. Plagued by an itching beneath his skin, Dewey is inside, trying to scratch himself better. He covers himself with calamine lotion but the itching doesn't stop. He tries everything. Cough mixture. Hydrogen peroxide. Nothing works. Then he catches sight of his face in the mirror. Small black flies are crawling out of his skin. Desperate for relief, Dewey grabs a bottle of insecticide and drinks the lot. When his friend Nat Heller comes to persuade Dewey to go surfing, it is already too late.

A day later, Loengard and Sayers arrive in Los Angeles. They haven't been to California since they graduated from UCLA and headed straight for Washington DC. Now they are returning for their friend Dewey's funeral. However, when they get to Nat Heller's house, which Dewey once shared, they think they might have made a mistake. A party is in full flow. Heading inside, they discover that Nat is actually throwing a wake for Dewey.

A friend of Loengard's from UCLA, Nat has dropped out of his graduate marine-biology program to work as a life-guard. He doesn't seem to want to talk about Dewey so Loengard and Nat head for the waves and go surfing. Sayers stays behind in the house where she takes a call from a Mr. Whitman at the funeral home that is holding Dewey's body. Mr. Whitman tells Sayers that some men from the County Coroner's Office have come to take Dewey's body away with them. Before Sayers can find out exactly what is going on, the line goes dead.

1952, Ohio, United States
Air Force pilots on UFO missions from Wright-Patterson Air Force Base were given instructions to shoot down any unfamiliar craft.

Sayers smells a rat and goes to the funeral home to investigate herself. As she arrives she is caught on a black and white film being taken by a mystery cameraman. Inside the funeral home she discovers that she is too late. Dewey's body has already been removed. Mr. Whitman explains that the men threatened to quarantine his whole establishment if he didn't comply with their demands. As a reason, they told Mr. Whitman that the chemicals Dewey had ingested would make the cremation of his body a hazard.

Back on the beach, Loengard and Nat have a heart to heart. Nat talks about the pressure to marry he is getting from his girlfriend Gina. Then finally he starts to open up about Dewey's death. Nat thinks that Dewey might have been under pressure from his work as an intern at the local hospital.

Walking back to her car on her way from the funeral home, Sayers catches sight of a man filming her in the rear-view mirror of her car. Unseen, she sneaks up behind him with her gun and demands to know what he is doing. A few questions quickly reveal that the young man is nothing to do with Majestic or the Hive. He is Jim Morrison, a film student at UCLA.

That night, Sayers tells Loengard about Morrison while they are strolling along the beach. Morrison has been filming around the beach for weeks and Sayers thinks he may have got a shot of the men who took Dewey's body. Then, suddenly, their attention is drawn to something small and shimmering which flies out of the water to land on the sand in front of them. When they stop to look properly, they see that the entire cove has been covered by a shimmering blanket of fish. They are literally hurling themselves out of the sea.

Next day the beach is closed, and the official line is that

there has been a spill of raw sewage from the local treatment plant. Loengard is not convinced. He asks Nat to do an autopsy on one of the dead fish found on the beach. Nat isn't keen but he is persuaded to go along with Loengard's request by his girlfriend, Gina. Meanwhile, Jim Morrison shows up. He wants to show Sayers the whole of his experimental film about decay.

Morrison takes Sayers to a UCLA screening room and begins the film. They wade through images of the ocean, a dead seagull and an obese tourist before Morrison captures a boat containing two fishermen. One dips a net into the water and pulls out a thrashing fish. The other dips some kind of thin rod into the fish's mouth and reads the rod before throwing the fish back into the sea. The next time the peculiar fishermen appear in the film, they are wheeling Dewey's body out of the funeral home. Morrison has already checked the men out and discovered that they are not from the Coroner's office but treatment plant employees.

Meanwhile Nat has taken a look at the fish and apart from a bacterial film across its eyes which was probably caused by the spill, he can find nothing wrong with it. Certainly no reason why it should have thrown itself out of the sea. When Loengard insists that there must be something, Nat accuses him of having forgotten how to have fun.

That night, Loengard joins Sayers and Morrison on a trip to the sewage treatment plant. They enter via a drainage pipe which is only supposed to be used during heavy rainfall. The plant calls it the "emergency discharge" route and the sewage which runs out through this pipe does not pass through any chemical treatments.

Loengard climbs through an access porthole in the pipe to take a look at the plant itself. He sees the aeration basins and several shipping crates full of empty jars before a pair of feet appear in view just a little too close for comfort. Loengard then catches a few words of the plant worker's conversation. "Lo'op a. Zhoo mum lu thirteen." It's clear that the plant worker is Hive.

Loengard quickly climbs back down into the tunnel, just in time to hear the rumble of water gathering behind them. Morrison, Loengard and Sayers are blasted out of the emergency discharge tunnel on a river of untreated sewage.

PLANET EARTH TIMELINE

Inexplicable

18 November 1952 Rear-Admiral Hillenkoetter sent a briefing document to President-elect Dwight Eisenhower outlining the activities of Majestic-12 since 1947.

Back at Nat's house, Loengard and Sayers decide to analyse some of the water with which they have been drenched. When Nat catches them examining a sample with his equipment he is angry, but realising that he might be overreacting because of a row with Gina, he relents and shows Loengard that he has been examining the sample on too low a magnification. When he examines the slide himself, Nat sees plenty of the bacteria known as giardia, which he puts down to the sewage spill, but then he sees something that is not quite so common. It is a perfectly round micro-organism. Impossibly perfect. And it is feeding on the bacteria. Loengard and Sayers take a look, not understanding the significance of their find until Nat explains that this particular micro-organism is synthetic.

Suddenly it dawns on Sayers and Loengard that this synthetic bacteria eater must be something to do with the Hive, though as a method of implantation it would be horribly inefficient if it was also the cause of the fish committing suicide. Whatever the real story, they know that the organism must be originating in the treatment plant. They hook up with Jim Morrison again to see if his film of the treatment plant's official PR tour can offer them any clues. As they watch the film, they see plant workers loading jars which they believe must contain the micro-organism into crates to be shipped all over the world.

Down on the beach that day, Nat also gets a nasty surprise when he finds Dewey's body washed up in the surf. Not only has Dewey's body been dumped, his kidneys have been removed with surgical precision. When Nat returns to the house to find Sayers and Loengard, he then discovers his girlfriend Gina trying to cut off her forearm. Where they can see only the scratches Gina has inflicted on herself, she can see maggots crawling in her flesh. Loengard and Sayers suggest that this is the work of the virus and the only way to save Gina is to clear her body of the bacteria the virus survives on, by flooding Gina's system with antibiotics.

While Nat tries to save Gina, Loengard and Sayers go back

to the plant with Jim Morrison. There, Loengard manages to steal the keys to the truck loaded with the virus while Morrison and Sayers try to find a way to put the untreated sewage through chemical processing. Loengard is attacked by one of the plant workers and it seems that all may be about to be lost when a mystery gunman takes Loengard's attacker out. It is a Majestic agent. Albano. He sends his men into the plant while he talks to Sayers and Loengard.

21 January 1952, Washington DC, United States Truman's budget allocated 75% of all available funds to arms.

It turns out that Majestic knew about the Hive's plan to dump the synthetic virus into the ocean. The intention of the exercise was to make the human race part of the Hive's food chain by altering human body chemistry. Loengard insists that people need to know about what might have already been dumped in the ocean, to which Albano replies enigmatically, "We've got it covered."

On a different beach the next day, Loengard and Sayers discuss a tiny article on the last page of the newspaper. It says that 1700 tonnes of DDT have been dumped in the bay. A chemical company has taken the blame, but Loengard suspects that Majestic might have been "spot-cleaning the ocean." Unfortunately, while the DDT may have killed the Hive virus, it will also cause untold damage to the delicate ecology of the ocean.

Loengard takes one last surfing trip with Nat before he and Sayers have to move on. Out in the waves, they sit on their boards and cast Dewey's ashes onto the water. A surfer's funeral.

Nat and Gina decide to stay on in Los Angeles and Bach promises they will come to no harm if they do not talk about what they have witnessed. Jim Morrison however will not be kept quiet. Albano and his lackeys confiscate Morrison's camera but as Loengard says, Jim Morrison soon found a different medium through which to explore his truths.

MUSIC
Surfer Girl by The Beach Boys
Surf City by Jan and Dean

See:
Abbott, Gina — Morrison, Jim — Dewey — UCLA
Heller, Nat — Whitman

The Enemy Within

WRITER
Brad Markowitz

DIRECTOR
Jim Charleston

GUEST STARS
Dorie Barton
Tim Kelleher
Kent McCord
Joan McMurtrey
Sean O'Bryan
Conor O'Farrell
Terry Bozeman
Tim Choate
Mike Kennedy

CO-STARRING
Deputy : Ed Beichner
Waitress : Annie O'Donnell
Earl Jarvis : Don Pugsley
Young Ray : Tyler Inices
Young Loengard : Antony Medwetz
Cooper : Terry Woodberry

Fresno, August 19th, 1964. Ray Loengard is enjoying a quiet night in his tent on a camping trip when he is woken by the wind outside the tent stirring up a storm. Before he knows what is happening, the tent is suddenly whipped up into the sky and Ray is left exposed to the elements. But this is no natural accident caused by the weather. In the forest before him, Ray sees the silhouette of a humanoid creature with an oversized head. The creature approaches him, proffering some kind of pod. It is an organic freeze pod that quickly immobilises the stricken camper. Ray Loengard has been visited by the Grays.

Later that year, in November, Kimberley Sayers and John Loengard are planning a trip back to Loengard's family home

in Fresno. They are fast running out of money and Loengard hopes to be able to cash in some of the bonds that his father has been keeping for him. However, when they reach Loengard's home, his family seem a little distant. Loengard thinks that they are probably worried for him, living on the road as he does, but his brother Ray seems particularly hostile. Loengard's sister Lucy tells Sayers that she thinks that Ray is moody because he is jealous of his younger brother. She dates the start of his jealousy back to a day when, as a child, Loengard saved Ray from drowning in the river near their home.

Back at Majestic HQ, Steele has managed to infiltrate the records office. Going through the files, he finds Loengard's details, which include the address of his family home. Steele is discovered by Albano, but comes off best in the ensuing gun-fight. Bach and his men go in search of Steele who is able to cope with his injuries because he feels no pain. When Bach discovers that Steele has taken Loengard's files, he decides it is time to bring Loengard in. Steele meanwhile hides out in the washrooms and starts to stitch his own wounds.

At the Loengard homestead, Loengard finds Ray rooting through his car and instinctively pulls a gun on him. Disturbed at this turn of events, Dick Loengard, the brothers' father, tells John that he will have to dump the gun for as long as he intends to stay with his family.

Later that day, Ray goes to sit alone by the river and think things over. While he is there, he has a vivid memory of the day he almost drowned, and of Loengard pulling him to safety.

Loengard follows Ray and joins him there, hoping to make amends. However, Loengard is taken aback when Ray says, "Ray Loengard wants you to stay", referring to himself in the impersonal third person. Picking up on this peculiarity of speech, Loengard attempts an EBE profile by asking Ray if he remembers some aspects of their childhood. The phrases Loengard uses are ridiculous, but Ray responds as if Loengard were talking sense. As far as Loengard is concerned, this is clear evidence that his brother has been infiltrated by the Hive.

21 January 1952, New York City, United States Thirteen communists were convicted of conspiring to teach and advocate the overthrow of the United States government by force.

Back at home, Loengard asks his sister whether Ray has been on one of his camping trips lately. She responds that indeed he has. In fact, Ray came back a day late from the last trip. Loengard decides that they may have to ART Ray. When he and Sayers track Ray down to the garage, they discover him listening to a Hive broadcast on the radio. They grab him, certain now that an ART is essential, but before Loengard can administer the chemicals, his father intervenes. Loengard tries to explain the circumstances to his father, but Dick is understandably unconvinced by the implantation story.

Loengard tells his father the whole story. He even tells him about the involvement of President Kennedy. But Dick just can't believe him. Dick tells Loengard that he will have the bonds Loengard wanted cashed but then Loengard and Sayers must leave. However, the next morning at the bank, Loengard is surprised by Sheriff Earl Jarvis, who has come to take Loengard to the psychiatric ward of the local hospital on his father's orders.

Meanwhile Steele has escaped detection at Majestic headquarters and now he and Majestic are racing to be the first to find Loengard. Visiting the hospital where Loengard is being held, Sayers finds that Majestic are already there. Steele bypasses the hospital and steals a car to drive straight to the Loengard home. There he meets Ray and upon discovering that Ray is not ready to kill his brother, Steele decides it is time to introduce Ray to the sphere of light that will make him an unquestioning slave of the Hive.

Sayers helps Loengard escape the hospital by posing as his sister and they head for the Loengard home again to make one last attempt to tell their story. However, by the time they reach there, Dick Loengard is no longer the sceptic he once was, having discovered Steele's blood-stained car on his property, with Loengard's Majestic file discarded on the front seat. Reading that file, Dick Loengard realises that his son has been telling the truth. Majestic-12 does indeed exist.

PLANET EARTH TIMELINE

Inexplicable

14 July 1952, United States The crew of a Pan American Airlines DC-4 en route from New York to San Juan, Puerto Rico, encountered six glowing discs of approximately 100 feet in diameter approaching at speed.

They race to the river's edge where Steele is trying to force Ray to touch the sphere of light. Before the transaction can take place, Loengard interrupts. Steele however is still convinced that Ray will do his bidding and asks Ray to kill Loengard with his gun. Ray continues to resist. He seems able to block Steele's command only by thinking back to that day by the river when Loengard saved his life. Sensing a deadlock, Steele shoots Ray and then turns to shoot Loengard, but before he can do so, Steele himself is shot by Dick. Steele's body falls into the river and is quickly carried away. The survivors turn their attention back to Ray, but realise that he is dead when the ganglion that has been inhabiting his body evacuates itself.

Loengard cannot stay in Fresno to console his father. He has to flee to escape detection by Majestic who are almost certainly on their way. The story of the Loengard brothers seems to have come full circle. Once John Loengard saved Ray's life, now Ray has given up his life for John.

Back on the road again, Loengard and Sayers are tailed by a black car. This time, however, it is not Majestic but the Justice Department. They have come to take Loengard and Sayers to a meeting with Bobby Kennedy, the Attorney General.

Actress Megan Ward has this to say of Sayers and Loengard in *The Enemy Within*: "*We learn we can never go home again, as much as we may think we can shield our loved ones from knowing the truth. It is a slow process of people becoming individually volunteers in the resistance.*"

See:
Abduction experiences — Loengard, Jo — Aker, Chet
Loengard, Lucy — ART — Loengard, Ray — EBE Profile
Organic Freeze Orbs — Gale, Dr. Jeffrey
Loengard, Dick

MILITARY INSTALLA
OFF LIMITS TO
UNAUTHORIZE
PERSONNEL

EPISODE TWELVE
The Warren Omission

WRITERS
Bryce Zabel & Brent V Friedman

DIRECTOR
Perry Lang

GUEST STARS
Jeri Lynn Ryan
Jay Acovone
Dennis Creaghan
James F Kelly
Gary Lockwood
Conor O'Farrell
Drew Snyder
Arthur Taxier
Wayne Tippit
Susan Griffiths
Mike Kennedy

CO-STARRING
Captain Norman Schwarzkopf : Gunther Jensen
Clyde Tolson : Jack Ritschel

In a safe house outside Bethesda, Maryland, Loengard and Sayers await a meeting with Attorney-General Robert "Bobby" Kennedy. When he arrives, he brings news that the Warren Commission is about to declare that Lee Harvey Oswald acted alone in the assassination of his brother, President John F Kennedy. Now Bobby has decided that Loengard will have to testify to the Commission to stop the truth about his brother's death from being lost forever. Sayers is hostile to the idea, thinking that Kennedy is using them, but later that night she agrees with Loengard's decision to testify. Bringing out the truth about the Hive is, after all, what they set out to do.

Next morning, Sayers and the justice agents guarding the safe house are surprised by a knock at the door. As agent

Barrett answers the knock, he is met with a swift side kick to the head. His assailant, a beautiful young woman, known only as Juliet, then deals out the same treatment to Barrett's colleague Kincaid before she knocks Sayers out with a blast from a Forced Consciousness Repressor.

16 July 1952,
Massachusetts,
United States
Four UFOs flying
in formation
above Salem,
Massachusetts, were captured on film
by a cameraman from the US
Coastguard.

When Loengard arrives to see what the commotion is about, dressed only in a towel, Juliet tells him she has a message for him: "You try to be a hero today, and I'll find you again. And next time we won't be talking." To underline her message she delivers a swift kick to Loengard's groin before robbing him of the towel he is wearing. She is obviously Majestic.

Loengard goes ahead with his testimony anyway, in front of a Commission which includes Chief Justice Earl Warren, Representative Gerald Ford, former CIA head Allen Dulles, Senators Russell and Cooper and General Counsel Lee Rankin. Loengard is introduced by Bobby Kennedy who describes the meeting which took place at his Hickory Hill Mansion before JFK was assassinated (see *The Awakening*). Then Loengard begins his testimony by describing that morning's threatening encounter with Juliet, before he takes the Commission back to the time when Loengard and Sayers first moved to Washington and Loengard was assigned to debunking Project Blue Book.

Allen Dulles, a member of the Warren Commission and the board of Majestic-12, tries to damage Loengard's credibility by describing his testimony as "some cockamamie story about little green men" but Loengard is allowed to continue. He describes how his investigation took him to meet Betty and Barney Hill, who were the first documented case of alleged abduction by aliens, and how that meeting led to his first unfriendly encounter with Captain Bach. When Bach is brought into the picture, Dulles again threatens Loengard, this time telling him that he is perjuring himself.

At Majestic headquarters, Albano and Bach are listening in on every word of the Commission's hearing but Bach is unworried by Loengard's accusations and says of Loengard that "He's digging his own grave", since he has no physical evidence or corroborating testimony. Albano is more cautious and suggests that they dig up some dirt on Loengard just in case.

Loengard has now moved on to talking about the formation of Majestic-12 and his recruitment to the agency by Bach himself. He recalls his first assignment, at the farm in Idaho where Patient Zero, Elliot Grantham, was found – the first human being to have been discovered to be hosting a ganglion. He describes how Majestic agent Jim Steele subsequently became infected by the same ganglion and arranged the killing of Lee Harvey Oswald by Jack Ruby on the orders of the Hive.

Rankin interrupts, saying that Loengard's testimony is nothing but an embarrassment and Warren has to agree. Bobby Kennedy goes to John's defence by saying that both he and his brother have seen physical evidence of the truth of Loengard's claims which leads Warren to close that day's hearing with a demand that that evidence be produced and Captain Bach also be brought in for questioning.

When Bach takes the stand he tries to claim that Loengard is "not playing with a full deck." Bach claims that it was Loengard who attacked him at gunpoint and tried to blackmail his way into Majestic to get incriminating material on the congressman he was working for. When Warren asks about the nature of Majestic, Bach avoids probing questions by saying that he cannot discuss Majestic without an Executive Order, something which Warren does not have.

Faced with Bach's denial of Loengard's role in Majestic, Bobby Kennedy calls up the fact that Loengard was on the payroll of a non-existent pet store, called The Aquarium, which was used as a Majestic front. Warren takes note of this evidence but Loengard is soon plunged deeper into disrepute when Bach suggests that Congressman Pratt, who was a Hive implantee, was pushed to suicide by Loengard's blackmail. According to Bach, Loengard obtained a negative psychiatric evaluation of Pratt and used this to get Sayers a job at the White House.

Further to this, Bach describes the day when Sayers and Loengard broke into his house to steal the artefact he used to keep around his neck, except that he doesn't tell Warren about the artefact, rather he says that Loengard stole some money and his Majestic ID. This robbery, claims Bach, led Majestic to make moves to investigate Loengard but they were beaten to it by Loengard's own family, who had him committed to a mental ward, where he was diagnosed as a paranoid schizophrenic with a Kennedy obsession. He even goes so far as to implicate Loengard in the murder of his brother Ray before delivering his coup de grace. Bach finally tells Warren, "you might also want to investigate his whereabouts on November 22nd", which was of course the day of JFK's assassination.

PLANET EARTH
TIMELINE
Inexplicable

July 1952,
Veronica,
Argentina
The residents of
Veronica,
Argentina witnessed six discs circling above the town, then disappearing into the night sky. This sighting occurred within hours of a similar report by Captain Paul Carpenter near Denver. Carpenter estimated that the craft must have been travelling at 3,000 miles per hour, making it possible for the saucers to have appeared in both locations at the reported times.

The commission is closed for recess over the weekend, with Loengard and Bach held in custody until it reconvenes. Outside the court, Sayers meets with Kennedy to suggest how they might be able to save Loengard from being charged with perjury.

Later that night, Majestic HQ is wracked by an explosion. Armed men storm the corridors and take out a Majestic agent who stands in their way. Bobby Kennedy follows the intruders, who are in fact Justice department agents, into the control room where they persuade one Norman Schwarzkopf to let them into the vault where the classified material is kept.

In that vault, Juliet, the woman who dealt Loengard such a cruel blow the other morning, is helping Albano to shred secret documents. Hearing Kennedy and his men approach, Albano sends Juliet to see J. Edgar Hoover. She slips out through a side door as Kennedy enters the vault and has Albano restrained while the Justice agents blow open the Majestic safe.

Back in the holding cell, Loengard and Bach have a strained conversation. Loengard warns his adversary that Bobby Kennedy will be president one day, to which Bach replies prophetically, "That man will never become President". While they are talking, a guard tells Bach that his lawyer has arrived. It is Juliet. She warns Bach that the office has been closed down and advises him that she will be paying a social call on J. Edgar Hoover.

Minutes later, J. Edgar Hoover wakes to find a woman in his bedroom. It is Juliet, of course. She tells him that she is looking for a "home movie" as discussed with Albano in Mississippi after Hoover objected to the burning of a church that was being used as a Hive nursery. While Hoover tells Juliet what he thinks of her (she's a "piece of garbage"), they are interrupted by another man. His name is Clyde Tolson and he shares Hoover's home.

Hoover knows he is stuck now. He knows that he will have to give Juliet what she is looking for or face having his private life held up for public scorn. Hoover directs Juliet to his underwear drawer, where she finds a spool of film. Unwinding it, she smiles at the images, saying, "they made such a happy couple."

Back at Majestic HQ, Bobby Kennedy has what he wants. It is an enhanced film of his brother's assassination. As the first two shots are fired, the driver of the car turns towards the President and a flash of light is seen to come from his sleeve, implying that the driver was the "third shooter". Bobby wants to present this evidence to the

Commission but before he can do that, Juliet arrives with a film of her own. Bobby Kennedy watches in horror as Juliet plays a black and white film, taken from a security camera, of Bobby Kennedy with a beautiful blonde. The blonde is dead film star Marilyn Monroe. To make things worse, Juliet lets Bobby know that the film can be authenticated as having been shot on the day that Monroe died, raising questions about her so-called suicide.

Bobby Kennedy knows that the film could ruin his Senate campaign. To keep the story quiet, Albano demands that Bobby drop his accusations of conspiracy and retire from his position as Attorney-General to a nice Majestic property in New York. Albano hands Bobby an affidavit. He has no choice but to sign it.

Loengard finds out about Bobby Kennedy's desertion when Justice Agent Barrett reads out a prepared statement at the Warren Commission, in which the Attorney-General withdraws his sponsorship of Loengard and apologises for ever having brought him before the Commission. In his exasperation, Loengard accuses Bach of arrogance and exposes Dulles as a Majestic board member. He reminds Chief Justice Warren that "If you won't see the truth, or if you find it but hide it from the people, then the future is dark for all of us." Then Loengard leaves. His testimony has not convinced Warren but it does lead Gerald Ford to suggest that too many questions have been raised for him to sign the Commission's report unless Bach makes a full disclosure about the nature of Majestic-12. Bach agrees, but only if he can talk to Warren alone.

Alone with Warren, Bach admits that Majestic does exist and that it was indeed created by President Truman in 1947, but he categorically denies that Roswell had anything to do with aliens. Bach claims that the Roswell Incident occurred when an elite group of Soviet commandos nearly got away with two US hydrogen bombs. Since that day, Majestic-12's mission has been to keep the Cold War cold. With regard to JFK's assassination, Bach admits that a Majestic man tailing Kennedy turned out to be a communist. Warren wants to report this to the Commission but Bach swiftly puts a stop to that by warning him that by revealing the "true" nature of Majestic and Kennedy's communist killer, he will be inviting atomic war. Warren concedes and when Bach returns to Majestic HQ, he is greeted with a standing ovation from his colleagues for his amazing gall.

Discredited and disillusioned, Sayers and Loengard are taken home. When Justice agent Barrett drops them off, he tries to press an envelope of cash onto Loengard. It is from the Attorney-General. Loengard doesn't want to be bought off, but Sayers accepts the money so that they can continue their mission to bring Majestic-12 to justice once and for all.

The Warren Commission eventually releases its report. They conclude that Lee Harvey Oswald acted alone and that there was no conspiracy, either domestic or international. Loengard's testimony does not appear in the report.

See:

Barrett, George — Kennedy, John F
Schwarzkopf, Captain Norman — Boggs, Representative
Kennedy, Robert — Third Shooter — Cooper, Senator
McCloy — Tolson, Clyde — Dulles, Allen
Monroe, Marilyn — Warren, Earl
Forced Consciousness Repressor
Oswald, Lee Harvey — Juliet — Ford, Gerald
Pratt, Charles — Roswell Incident
Hoover, J. Edgar — Rankin, Lee

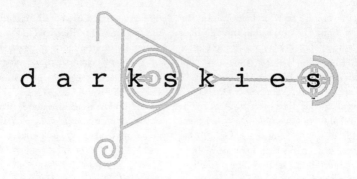

THE ENCYCLOPAEDIA
OF
DARK SKIES

ABBOTT, GINA

A friend of Loengard and Sayers from their days as students at UCLA. Gina is the girlfriend of Nat Heller, a drop-out marine biologist. (The Last Wave).

ABDUCTION EXPERIENCES

(See Betty and Barney Hill, Hypnagogic State)

AKER, CHET

Manager of the Fresno bank where Dick Loengard had his son John Loengard arrested and taken to hospital for a mental health checkup. (The Enemy Within).

ALBANO, PHIL

A Majestic agent. Captain Frank Bach's sidekick.

ALMA

A Las Vegas matron who was winning big bucks at the $100 blackjack table when Kim Sayers served her a drink and experienced the Buzz that told her Alma was Hive. (Dreamland).

AMYGDALA

One of the most evolutionarily ancient parts of the human central nervous system. The amygdala is the part of the brain that controls our emotional responses. The ganglion uses the human amygdala as a base from which to begin its take-over of a host.

THE APOLLO MISSIONS

The famous Apollo missions of the 1960's and 1970's were ended abruptly after the flight of Apollo 17. An unofficial report by Maurice Chatelain (an ex-NASA scientist) contained the news that all the Apollo missions had been followed, "both at a distance but also sometimes quite closely, by space vehicles of extra-terrestrial origin."

The Apollo landings supposedly sent back live broadcasts but it has subsequently been revealed that the "live broadcast" in fact had a ten-second delay built in so that Mission Control could censor the news coming through. The astronauts also employed code, as suggested by the seemingly nonsensical references to "Barbara".

All the Apollo missions reported the incidence of inexplicable phenomena. Apollo 11 picked up an unexplained radio transmission. Apollo 12 was hit by a bolt of "lightning" on take-off, though there was no storm for miles around the launch pad. Later, Apollo 12 also picked up peculiar radio transmissions. Apollo

16 reported a bizarre flash of light and on the final Apollo flight, the command module pilot reported sighting a flashing light in the Crater Orientale. Immediately after this, the pilot switched his broadcast back to Mission Control into code saying: "Kilo, kilo. Select OMNI."

Dr. Farouk El Baz, another ex-NASA scientist, reported that "not every discovery has been announced" while his colleague Dr. F. Bell admitted that "astronauts have kept silent about UFO encounters because they are trained to believe that it is a matter of national security."

NASA science writer and amateur radio hack Otto Binder claimed that he was able to get hold of some of the secrets of the Apollo launches anyway. He managed to bypass Mission Control's broadcast delay and picked up the following dialogue between astronauts Aldrin and Armstrong and Mission Control:

Armstrong: "What was it? What the hell was it? That's all I want to know . . ."
Aldrin: "I'm telling you there are other spacecraft out there . . . lined up on the far side of the crater edge . . . they're on the moon watching us."

One explanation is that this particular Apollo mission had stumbled across the wreckage of the Soviet launch "Vostok". But since Vostok wasn't supposed to have been able to make it as far as the moon, the real identity of "they" is still unknown. (Mercury Rising).

AREA 51

A legendary top-secret military installation, rumoured to be the place where the spacecraft remains recovered during the Roswell Incident are now kept. In reality, Area 51 is a small area of land inside Nellis Air Force Base, in the Nevada desert. It can be found near Groom Lake, a dry basin concealed by a range of low hills, patrolled by security guards in camouflage gear and marked only by a series of widely-spaced orange poles.

Allegedly the site at Groom Lake, which consists of a few buildings and an extremely long runway, has been used as a testing ground for top-secret aircraft for the past 40 years. The first U2 planes were tested there and it has been rumoured that alien technology was

re-engineered at Area 51 from plans made using the craft found at Roswell. This rumour is supported by the testimony of physicist Bob Lazar, who in 1989 claimed that he had worked on extraterrestrial craft at a place called "Papoose Lake", just south of Area 51. (Unfortunately, while Bob Lazar's claims about Area 51 have yet to be contradicted, his personal credentials, including his having been educated at Cal-tech and MIT, have yet to be confirmed.)

Area 51 was also known as "Dreamland". (Hostile Convergence, Dreamland).

ART

In response to MJ-12's gruesome and always fatal "cerebral eviction" practice, ART, the Alien Rejection Technique, was developed by Majestic's Doctor Carl Hertzog as a saner and safer method of removing ganglions from human hosts implanted by the Hive.

Loengard became the first practitioner of ART (an "artist") when he employed the experimental technique under field conditions on his girlfriend, Kimberley Sayers. Also known as "saving", ART can take up to 4 hours. The method employs various toxic chemicals, taken orally, to alter the PH balance of the host's body, thus making it an unsuitable environment for the ganglion. This is followed by an injection of acetone, the main ingredient in nail polish remover. ART boasts a survival rate of 50% if performed during the early stages of implantation. During the final moments of ART, the human host coughs up the ganglion which is capable of surviving outside a host for up to an hour. (The Awakening, We Shall Overcome, The Enemy Within).

AUGATREUX, GARY

A pilot in NASA's covert operation, Midnight Wing, Augatreux flew on the "unmanned" Gemini mission which encountered the Grays' mother ship, thought at the time to be a Soviet satellite known as the "Black Knight". Requested by NASA to fire on the "Knight", Augatreux's mission was interrupted by a blinding flash. When Augatreux was next able to see, he discovered that Gemini's clock gave a reading of two hours later and, looking out of the window, he saw that he was on the other side of the earth. Augatreux had in fact been abducted from his craft and implanted with a ganglion before being returned to Gemini. Fortunately, Augatreux's condition was discovered before he was able to sabotage a second flight at the Hive's behest. (Mercury Rising).

BACH, CAPTAIN FRANK

Head of the mysterious Majestic-12 agency. Frank Bach was appointed to the leadership of Majestic-12 by President Truman, who admired Bach's intuitive handling of the Roswell Incident.

BACH, JENNIFER

Seven-year-old daughter of Captain Frank Bach. (Inhuman Nature).

BACH, MRS.

Frank Bach's wife. Bach kept his wife in the dark about the real nature of his work with Majestic-12. (The Awakening, Inhuman Nature).

BAINBRIDGE, ALICIA

Sayers' supervisor in the First Lady's Office at the White House. (Moving Targets).

BALFOUR, CLARK

Balfour was a radar controller present at Roswell on the night of July 1947 when President Truman met the Grays' deposition. Later, Balfour helped Majestic to set up his old colleague Jesse Marcel and Loengard, by giving them the key to a box containing fake UFO plans as part of his "dying" wish to be absolved for his part in the Roswell cover-up. (Moving Targets & Hostile Convergence).

BALFOUR, KATE

Wife of Clark Balfour. Kate helped Clark to set up Jesse Marcel and Loengard. (Hostile Convergence).

BARRETT, GEORGE

A high-level Justice agent assigned by the Attorney-General to protect Sayers and Loengard while they awaited Loengard's appearance in front of the Warren Commission. (The Warren Omission).

BARROW, REV. GARY

A Christian minister from Chiliwack, Alaska. Reverend Gary Barrow was the nephew of Tug Barrow, descended from the Tlingit Indians of Alaska. (Ancient Future).

BARROW, TUG

A Tlingit Indian shaman who saw the floating rocks in the mountains near Chiliwack, Alaska. Tug was the keeper of the story of the "Star which fell from the Sky." (Ancient Future).

BAY OF PIGS

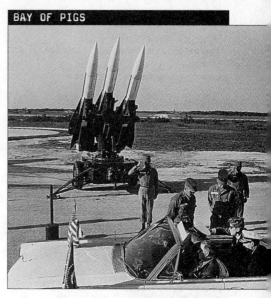

The first fiasco of the Kennedy administration. The Bay of Pigs affair refers to a US invasion gone wrong in the Cuban bay of the same name. The US had been waiting to take action on Cuba since Marxist dictator Fidel Castro took over the island in 1959. In 1961, a small force of CIA-trained Cuban exiles was landed at the Bay of Pigs from US ships but they were swiftly captured by Castro's troops. The whole affair was a huge embarrassment to Kennedy and only seemed to strengthen both Castro's regime and his links with the Soviet Union.

THE BEATLES

Arguably the most famous band in the whole world, The Beatles took America by storm in the early 1960's. The "fab four" were John Lennon on guitar, Paul McCartney on bass,

22 August 1952
A memo from George Carey (Assistant Director of Operations, CIA) to Allen Dulles (Deputy Director of Intelligence) informed him that the Soviets had explained away UFOs in their territory as tools put into the air by the US Naval Research Bureau for the purposes of stratospheric research.

1952, United States
President Eisenhower was elected to office.

19 September 1952, RAF Dishforth, England
In a clear sky, a UFO was seen to follow a Meteor jet approaching RAF Dishforth, in an incident which, according to Blue Book chief Ed Ruppelt, caused the RAF to officially recognise the existence of UFOs.

1953, Moscow, USSR
Soviet Premier Josef Stalin died. Stalin was succeeded by Nikita Khruschev.

1953, Moscow, USSR
The KGB, the Soviet equivalent of the CIA, was formed.

George Harrison on lead guitar and Ringo Starr on drums. All four of the band members sang as well, creating that unmistakable "Mersey Sound".

The Beatles' first appearance on American television came on January 3rd 1964, when they appeared on NBC-TV's "Jack Paar Show". It wasn't a live performance, but a clip taken from a BBC program called "The Mersey Sound" on which they sang "She loves you."

Less than a fortnight later, The Beatles broke into the US chart with "I want to hold your hand", which became the fastest ever UK million seller, reaching number one on February 1st 1964 and staying at the top of the charts for almost three months.

On February 7th 1964, The Beatles finally arrived in the United States in person. Their Pan-Am flight PA 101 touched down at JFK airport at 1.20 EDT. They were greeted by hordes of screaming girls thanks to the busy publicity people at Capitol Records who had spent weeks whipping America into a Beatles frenzy despite the fact that Capitol had turned down The Beatles' first four singles.

The Beatles were in New York to make a live appearance on the Ed Sullivan Show. When the show was aired on February 9th, the US Police Force reported a marked drop in crime figures while 73 million Americans settled down to watch. That night, The Beatles performed five songs: "All my loving", "Till there was you", "She loves you", "I saw her standing there" and "I want to hold your hand". (They did not play "Money (that's what I want)" as performed in Dark Skies' episode "Dark Day's Night".) The Beatles were paid $2,400.00 for their appearance on the show which also included as guests Georgia Brown and the children's chorus from a Broadway production of Oliver, featuring future "Monkees" frontman Davy Jones.

The American love affair with The Beatles continued until December 8th 1980, when crazed American fan Mark David Chapman gunned down John Lennon outside the Dakota Building, New York, which had been John's home for almost a decade. John died from a massive loss of blood at 11.30 in the Roosevelt Hospital. (Dark Day's Night).

BERKNER, DR. LLOYD

Dr. Lloyd Berkner was made Executive Secretary of the Joint Research and Development Board in 1946. Later he led the Weapons Systems Evaluation Group and was a member of the CIA's UFO-debunking "Robertson Panel". Berkner is also alleged to have been one of the twelve original directors of Majestic-12.

BLACK POWER MOVEMENT

The Black Power Movement was a militant approach to the problem of civil rights, founded in the 1960s. The BPM discouraged alliances with white liberals as a means of bringing about a change in civil rights law.

BLIPVERTS

During the 1960s, advertisers hit upon the idea of using subliminal messages to get their point across. Images of the products they wished to sell were spliced into feature films. Though the image actually appeared on the screen for just a fraction of a second, disappearing again so quickly that most people would claim not to have noticed it, the blipverts did seem to be able to encourage people to buy more of the products featured in the blips, such as popcorn and soft drinks. Because of their potential for serious misuse, blipverts were eventually banned. (Dark Day's Night).

BOEHM, KESTER

Owner of the ranch in Monticello, Wisconsin, where the Grays were found to be using cattle to incubate human babies. (Inhuman Nature).

BOEHM, MARIAN

Wife of Kester Boehm. (Inhuman Nature).

BOGGS, REPRESENTATIVE

Member of Congress's House of Representatives present at the hearing of the Warren Commission. (The Warren Omission).

BRONK, DR. DETLEV

A respected physiologist and biologist, Dr. Bronk was Chairman of the National Research Council and a member of the Medical Advisory Board of the Atomic Energy Commission when he allegedly became one of the twelve original directors of Majestic-12. Dr. Bronk is also alleged to have carried out an autopsy on the bodies recovered at Roswell, leading him to describe them as "EBEs" (Extraterrestrial Biological Entities).

BROWN, CLARICE

Owner of the Cape Canaveral Motel and Gift Shop that Loengard and Sayers stayed at while

January 1953, United States The Robertson Panel was formed On The Record by the CIA at the request of the White House, to investigated UFO phenomena. After twelve hours of meetings, the sceptical panel concluded that "there was no threat to national security". One member of the panel, Dr. Page, went on to say that "present astronomical knowledge of the solar system makes the existence of intelligent beings... quite preposterous." Despite Dr. Page's sceptical conclusion, the entire Robertson Panel report was not fully declassified until 1975.

14 March 1953, USSR
A United States aircraft was fired upon by Russian MIG fighter planes.

23 July 1953, United States J.J. O'Neill, amateur Inexplicable astronomer and science editor of the Herald Tribune, reported that he had seen a bridge spanning approximately 19km in the Mare Crisium on the surface of the moon. The sighting was confirmed by British astronomer H.P.Wilkins.

investigating Sayers' recurring dream of an astronaut. (Mercury Rising).

BROWN, GENERAL ARTHUR

One of the twelve directors of Majestic according to Dark Skies.

BURNSIDE, RON

Hiver who ran pseudo-experiments in New York as part of the Hive's plan to condition throwbacks to react to suicide-inducing stimuli spliced into The Beatles' set on the Ed Sullivan Show. (Dark Day's Night).

27 July 1953, Korea
The Korean War ended. An armistice was signed which split the country once more at a battle-line not far from the original boundary of 1948.

19 October 1953, United States
An American Airlines DC-6 en route to Washington DC was buzzed by a UFO, forcing pilot Captain Kidd to throw the plane into a dive.

3 November 1953, Kent, England
RAF Flying Officer T.S. Johnson and his navigator Flying Officer G. Smythe were flying a Vampire jet at an altitude of 20,000 feet near RAF West Malling in Kent. They reported an encounter with a stationary object which was hovering at a much higher altitude. The object was circular in appearance and gave off a bright light. While Johnson and Smythe encountered the object in the air, army radar at Lee Green in Kent had picked up a large echo on their radar coming from a direction commensurate with the airmen's later report. The radar echo was analysed by Sergeant H. Waller who concluded that the echo's origin was three or four times larger than the largest airliner in manufacture at that time.

23 November 1953, Michigan, United States
Air Defence command picked up the radar echo of a UFO in the vicinity of Soo Locks, Michigan. An F-89C Scorpion jet was scrambled immediately to intercept the craft and was tracked on radar until the UFO and plane's echoes merged and the Scorpion jet, piloted by Lt. Felix Moncla, disappeared without trace.

BURSUM, MAYOR HOLM

Mayor of Socorro, the little town in New Mexico where police officer Lonnie Zamora spotted a UFO. (Hostile Convergence).

BUSH, DR. VANNEVAR

Dr. Vannevar Bush was a respected American scientist who led the Manhattan Project which developed the first atomic bomb. He later became head of the Joint Research and Development Board, before he was allegedly recruited as one of the original twelve directors of Majestic-12. A memo from Rear Admiral Roscoe Hillenkoetter to President Eisenhower suggests that Dr. Bush also headed up the investigation into the wreckage found near Roswell, New Mexico.

BUZZ

Even after successful ART, residual ganglion tendrils can remain embedded inside a saved human brain. Though the residual ganglion matter cannot regenerate itself and cause a problem in that sense, the tendrils can act as latent antennae for the Hive's telepathic frequency. ART survivors, or Receivers as they have come to be known, find that they usually experience an unintelligible "buzz" in the proximity of a Hive member, although the signal source is rarely easily identifiable.

Though surviving an alien implantation undoubtedly causes great emotional turmoil, survivors have proved themselves invaluable in the war against the Hive, using the Buzz as an early warning system. (Dreamland).

BUZZWORMS

The Hive's only natural predator. These alien leech-like creatures survive by eating ganglions. Hive member Jim Steele used buzzworms to deal with troublesome implantees, such as Jack Ruby, who was slipped a buzzworm in a hot dog. Steele also tried to use the worms on Sayers to rid her of the ganglion tendrils remaining in her after ART so that she could be re-implanted. (Dreamland).

CAPITALISM

Capitalism refers to the system of economic organisation under which the means of production, distribution and exchange are privately owned by corporations or individuals, who trade without government intervention. It is the ideological opposite of Communism.

Capitalism in its purest form is actually rare in the twentieth century, with most capitalist societies being subject to a certain degree of government intervention and also having a "welfare state" for those people who cannot fend for themselves, thus making the society "welfare capitalist". The United States is one such society.

CASSIE

Hiver waitress in the Socorro diner who encouraged Sayers to attend her sister's wedding in Denver, then informed Jim Steele of Sayers' movements. (Hostile Convergence).

CASTRO, FIDEL

President Kennedy's nemesis, the Cuban leader Fidel Castro, couldn't have come from a more different family background. Castro was the son of an immigrant sugar cane planter. He joined the Cuban People's Party in 1947 at the tender age of 20 and rose swiftly to lead his first revolution in Santiago in 1953. Castro was jailed for the Santiago affair but during his exile in Mexico he banded together with guerrillas such as Che Guevara and planned a much more successful attack.

Castro led a march on the Cuban capital of Havana in December 1958 and by 1 January 1959, the corrupt puppet dictator, General Batista, had gone. Declaring himself the new prime minister, Castro aligned himself with the Soviet Union and began the association which would cause Kennedy such a headache when the Cuban Missile Crisis broke in 1963.

CENTRAL INTELLIGENCE AGENCY

Established by Congress in 1947, the CIA's work includes the gathering and evaluation of foreign intelligence, overseas counter-intelligence operations, and the organisation of secret political intervention in areas outside the jurisdiction of the USA. The large budget with which the CIA employs thousands of agents in every corner of the world is not subject to the scrutiny of Congress.

The CIA is split into four main departments: the Department of Operations, the Department of Science and Technology, the Department of Intelligence and the Department of Administration. These four branches report to the National Intelligence Council, who in turn report to the National Security Council and the President.

The head of the CIA, the Director of Central Intelligence (DCI), manages the entire community of intelligence agencies within the US government as well as being responsible for the CIA. His vast umbrella of control encompasses the Defense Intelligence Agency, the Departments of the Treasury, Energy and State, and the Federal Bureau of Investigation.

In 1953, Allen W. Dulles became the Director of the CIA. He used his position to involve the United States in right wing coups in Guatemala and Iran in 1953, and, under Dulles' leadership, the CIA also began the series of intelligence operations in the USSR that culminated in Francis Gary Powers' ill-fated U2 flight into Soviet airspace. It was the Powers debacle and the CIA's subsequent involvement with the disastrous Bay of Pigs incident that forced Dulles to resign in disgrace in 1961. He left the CIA facing serious questions about its future, but despite the misgivings of many in power, the CIA continued to maintain its controversial dual role at home and abroad.

CENTRAL NERVOUS SYSTEM

Comprising the brain and the spinal cord, the central nervous system allows signals from the brain to be passed throughout the body. A ganglion hijacks this system to spread its control throughout the body of a host.

CENTRAL TREATY ORGANISATION

In 1956, the USA joined a mutual security alliance between Britain, Turkey, Iran, Iraq and Pakistan, designed as a defence against the Soviet Union.

CHESNEY

Loengard and Sayers' open-minded Washington landlord. (The Awakening).

CLOAKERS

Majestic agents sent to "cloak" or cover up events which Majestic wish to remain a secret.

1954, Manila, The Philippines
The South-East Asia Treaty Organisation, a defence alliance between the USA, Australia, Britain, France, New Zealand, Pakistan, the Philippines and Thailand, was signed in Manila, as part of the US policy of containment of communism.

1954, Switzerland
The Geneva Conference saw the division of Vietnam into two states, a communist Democratic Republic in the north and a non-communist republic in the south.

21 January 1954, United States
The first atomic bomb was launched in Groton, Connecticut.

17 February 1954, United States
Commercial airline pilots were made subject to the same restrictions as military pilots with regard to reporting UFOs.

August 1954, United States
N.F. Twining, Chief of Staff, signed the USAF released document number 200-2, dealing with official procedures for reporting UFO sightings. The document states that:
"9. Release of Facts. Headquarters USAF will release summaries of evaluated data which will inform the public on this subject. In response to local inquiries, it is permissible to inform news media reporters on UFOs when the object is positively identified as a familiar object, except that the following type of data warrants protection and should not be revealed: Names of principals, intercept and investigation procedures and classified radar data. For those objects which are not explainable, only the fact that ATIC will analyse the data is worthy of release, due to the many unknowns involved."

COCHRAN

Head of the Hive gambling racket in Las Vegas, which was providing funds for the construction of an underground headquarters near Area 51. (Dreamland).

COLD WAR

Cold War is the term applied to the tension between the countries of the Soviet Bloc and those of the West which followed the end of World War II. Though the Soviet Union had been a wartime ally of Britain and the United States, differences between the nations began to arise over the future of the defeated Germany and Eastern Europe. When Eastern Europe fell into communist hands and Turkey and Greece looked set to go the same way, the West started to build its defences with steps such as the Truman Doctrine of 1947 and the Marshall Plan, which was supposed to bolster the economies of western Europe.

Four years after the end of World War II, the North Atlantic Treaty Organisation underlined the intention of the West to stand as one against possible attack, a move which was countered by the Soviet establishment of the "Council for Mutual Aid and Assistance" and the Warsaw Pact of 1955.

The Cold War was fought on many fronts, with the US standing against communism in Korea, Indo-China, Hungary and of course, most spectacularly, in Cuba and Vietnam. Tension was increased by the development of a nuclear arms race during the 1950s which escalated until the Cuban Missile Crisis of 1963 made clear the need for some kind of control on both sides. A modicum of sense seemed to enter the proceedings in 1963, with the signing of the Nuclear Test-ban treaty, but the Cold War continued in one form or another right up until the USSR held its first democratic elections in 1989.

COMINFORM

Cominform is the name of a modified form of Comintern, an alliance of Communist nations with the aim of world revolution. Comintern was established by Lenin in 1919. Cominform came into being in 1947, with a similar world view. It was dissolved in 1956.

COMMUNISM

Communism is a social and political ideology which advocates the importance of the community. Under communism, all property belongs to the community and each member of that community works for the common good according to his or her abilities and receives from the community according to his or her needs. Communism is the ideological opposite of Capitalism.

Communism entered the world political arena for real in 1917, when Lenin led his Bolsheviks (Russian for "Members of the Majority") in the Russian Revolution, overthrowing the Tsarist autocracy, and establishing in its place the Union of Soviet Socialist Republics.

CONGRESS

The Congress of the USA is the legislative branch of the US government. Congress is divided into two houses, the House of Representatives and the Senate. The House of Representatives has a membership system based on the population of each state with Representatives serving a two-year term, while the Senate, which is the higher of the houses, has two members per state regardless of the state's size. Senators serve a term of six years.

Congress is responsible for taxation, defence, welfare, the military, the postal service and federal courts. These are dealt with by standing committees who specialise in a certain area of policy.

CONTAINMENT

The name given to the most basic principle of US foreign policy since the end of World War Two. Containment refers to the "containment of Soviet expansionist tendencies" by the creation of such military pacts as NATO and SEATO, which were backed up with military force and nuclear missiles. During the 1960s the policy of containment was extended to cover Africa and Latin America, most notably Cuba.

COOPER, SENATOR

Senator present at the hearing of the Warren Commission at which Loengard testified against Majestic. (The Warren Omission).

23 August 1954, Vernon, France
Local businessman Bernard Miserey had just arrived home at one o'clock in the morning when he sighted a huge cigar-shaped object hovering silently above the River Seine. As Miserey watched, a horizontal disc shape seemed to drop from the bottom of the cigar. It grew bright, as if surrounded by a halo, hovering for a few minutes beneath the cigar, before it darted away at high speed. In all, five disc shapes fell from the cigar before the cigar simply faded away. When Miserey reported his encounter to the police, he was told that a policeman and an army engineer had both seen exactly the same thing.

11 October 1954, Essex, England
Flight Lieutenant James Salandin encountered 3 objects on a Meteor Mk. 8 flight from RAF North Weald in Essex. The objects were saucer shaped, one was gold, another silver. None of them seemed to have windows or portholes and none showed any obvious means of propulsion.

1955, United States
General MacArthur is believed to have been involved in the establishment of the Interplanetary Phenomenon Unit (IPU), an agency formed to investigate crashed and retrieved alien craft. In 1955 MacArthur stated that: "The nations of the world will have to unite for the next war will be an interplanetary war." This statement led to intense speculation that the IPU had uncovered more facts about UFOs than have subsequently been revealed.

1955, Warsaw, Poland
Eight Soviet bloc countries signed the Warsaw Pact as a response to the news that West Germany had been allowed to join NATO.

February 1955,
Hampshire,
England
A saucer and its
pilot were
alleged to have
landed on the country estate of Lord
Mountbatten at Broadlands, near Romsey
in Hampshire. The saucer was witnessed by a member of Mountbatten's
staff, Frederick Briggs, who said
that the encounter threw him from his
bicycle, which was then pinned on top
of him by some mysterious force.
Talking about the incident, Lord
Mountbatten is reported to have said
of the visitors: "They are far ahead
of us... If they really come over in
a big way that may settle the capi-
talist/communist war. If the human
race wishes to survive they may have
to band together."

4 October 1955, USSR
Three US officials, including Senator
Richard Russell and Lieutenant Colonel
E. Hathaway, spotted two discs taking
off almost vertically from a field
beside the railway track while they
were en route to Adzhijabul from
Atjaty. The CIA explained the phenomenon as high performance Soviet
aircraft.

1956, Ohio, United States
The University of Ohio picked up a
"code like radio chatter" from the
moon.

1956, Greenland
Valentin Akhuratov, Soviet Chief
Navigator on strategic ice reconnaissance near Cape Jesup in Greenland,
encountered a craft travelling at an
impossible speed which he described
as being like "a large pearl-covered
lens with wavy, pulsating edges".

CROP CIRCLES

One of Loengard's first missions for Majestic
was to investigate the appearance of a curious
glyph pattern in a wheat-field in Idaho. The
huge glyph, formed by flattened wheat, was literally in the middle of nowhere with no obvious entry or exit points that might suggest that
the shapes had been made by a car or truck.
The only explanation, it seemed, was that the
pattern must have been made from above.

The nature and position of the Idaho crop
circles suggested that the pattern indicated a
safe place for Hive ships to land. The discovery
of a golden delta shape set within the glyph
seemed to confirm this.

During the late 1980s and early 1990s, the
wheat-fields of the United Kingdom saw a
spate of the type of crop circles seen in Idaho.
Extensive scientific investigation suggested that
most of the British crop circles were the result
of freak weather conditions, like mini-cyclones,
that flattened the wheat in a strangely systemat-
ic manner. Many others were discovered to be
the work of clever pranksters.

CUBA

One of the largest Caribbean islands, Cuba
was a Spanish colony until US intervention in
1902 made it an independent republic. But it
has not had a happy history since independence and a series of corrupt governments,
which were often just puppets of American
interests, paved the way for Fidel Castro to
sweep to power in 1959.

CUBAN MISSILE CRISIS

The Cuban Missile Crisis was one of the most
frightening periods in modern world history. The
week of fear began in October 1962, when the
United States learned that Soviet missiles with
warheads capable of reaching the US mainland
were being installed in Cuba. In fact, there were
20,000 Russian troops on the island, supported
by 150 jets, 350 tanks and more than a thousand
guns and anti-aircraft missiles. Fortunately, the
warheads for the ballistic missiles, which gave the
US its biggest shock, did not yet seem to be in
place, giving President Kennedy a small breathing space in which to avert a crisis.

President Kennedy's first move was to rein-
force the US naval base at Guantanamo, order-
ing a naval blockade against Soviet shipments
to Cuba. He then went on national television to
demand that Krushchev and the Soviets withdraw their military presence from the island,

closing his speech with the provocative remark: "Our goal is not the victory of might, but the vindication of right."

The world held its breath and waited for nuclear war as both the United States and the Soviets went on full alert. Armageddon seemed frighteningly near when the US blockade was approached by Soviet vessels thought to be carrying missiles, though in fact they were simply merchant ships. Thankfully Krushchev ordered the Soviet ships to turn back before any shots were fired.

Five days after the crisis had begun, Krushchev sent an informal message to Kennedy, saying that the Soviets would withdraw from Cuba if the US would agree not to launch a subsequent invasion. Later that day, Krushchev made his proposition official.

The next day, however, Krushchev sent a new demand. The Soviet pullout from Cuba would depend upon a US pullout from Turkey. Though Kennedy had actually secretly ordered that the obsolete US missiles in Turkey be withdrawn months before the Cuban Missile Crisis flared up, Krushchev's cocky new tone was jarring. Kennedy was almost ready to launch an attack on Cuba to spite Krushchev when his brother, Robert Kennedy the Attorney-General, suggested that Kennedy send a message to Krushchev ignoring the Turkish issue altogether. At the same time, Robert Kennedy made an informal admission to the Soviet Ambassador that the US had wanted to remove its military presence from Turkey for months.

Krushchev's next message to Kennedy was a positive one. The Soviets would withdraw from Cuba. Two days later, the Cuban Missile Crisis was over. (The Awakening).

DALTON ROGERS, ARTHUR

A white supremacist. Sidekick of Clayton Lewis. (We Shall Overcome).

DARK SKIES

Founded by fugitives John Loengard and Kimberley Sayers, Dark Skies was formed as the unofficial response to the existence of the Hive on Earth. The actual phrase "Dark Skies" first came into use as a code-name coined when a member of the resistance discovered an out-

April 1956, Syracuse, United States
Flying back from Albany to Syracuse, Captain Raymond E. Ryan and his first officer, William Neff, encountered a brilliant white light, like an approaching aircraft burning landing lights, at a height of 6,000ft. However Ryan estimated that the object was moving at approximately 1,000 miles an hour - faster than any contemporary jet - and it glowed orange as it approached them. When Ryan and Neff reported the incident to Griffis Air Force base, members of the ground staff confirmed that they had also seen an orange object in the sky nearby. The sighting lasted for over twenty minutes.

13 August 1956, Bentwaters/Lakenheath, England
Three ground based radars used by the RAF/USAF at Bentwaters/Lakenheath made radio contact with a UFO. A confirmation on aerial radar by a Venom night fighter and nine visual sightings from the ground make this one of the most celebrated cases of modern times. The radar indicated that the objects were moving at up to 4,000 miles per hour - faster than any aircraft of the time could have achieved.

October 1956, Turkey
A US fixed-beam radar, situated on the coast of the Black Sea, beamed back evidence that the Soviets were developing ballistic missiles in Stalingrad.

break of the Hive and remarked that: "We're seeing a lot of dark skies over Kansas . . ."

Learning that Hives grow in small pockets simultaneously, Loengard and Sayers conceived a grass roots movement as the best method to tackle the spread. Dark Skies derived its power from its people-based response.

PLANET EARTH
TIMELINE
Inexplicable

6 November 1956, Ohio, United States
Olden Moore of Cleveland, Ohio claimed that he watched a landed UFO for as long as 20 minutes when it landed 30 miles to the east of Cleveland. Moore was taken for questioning and later claimed that he had spoken to unknown "high officials" in Washington who made him swear his story to secrecy.

10 February 1957, Iceland
Lieutenant Graham Bethune of the US Naval Reserve was flying from Keflavik in Iceland towards Argentia Naval Base in Newfoundland when he observed a reddish orange disc which he estimated to be at least 300 feet in diameter and travelling at more than 1,000 miles per hour.

4 April 1957, England
Five UFOs were tracked by radar equipment at RAF West Freugh. The incident sparked a twenty-four-hour watch by all radar stations.

31 May 1957, Kent, England
A British airliner passing over Rochester in Kent encountered a UFO which seemed to interfere with the plane's radio communications equipment.

17 July 1957, Texas, United States
An American Airlines flight to Dallas Texas, piloted by Captain Ed. Bachner, had a near collision with an object estimated to be the size of a B-47 100 miles east of El Paso, Texas.

September 1957, Ubatuba, Brazil
Material purported to be from a crashed flying saucer was analysed and found to be of magnesium so pure as to be beyond the production capabilities of any magnesium manufacture process known on Earth.

Dark Skies obtained US Government funding in 1981, only to be returned to the private sector again in 1989 under President Bush. This underground strike force has been responsible for saving, through the use of ART, over 50,000 human beings since 1963.

DE GAULLE, CHARLES ANDRÉ JOSEPH MARIE

President of France from 1959-1969, De Gaulle dominated the EEC during his reign. He was behind the development of an independent French nuclear deterrent and withdrew France from NATO in 1966. De Gaulle clashed with President Johnson over Vietnam in 1964, when De Gaulle asserted that Vietnam should remain a neutral territory. (Mercury Rising).

DEWEY

A friend of Sayers and Loengard from their days as students at UCLA. Dewey killed himself by drinking insecticide after becoming infected with a synthetic micro-organism which Hivers had been pumping into the sea along the coast of Los Angeles. (The Last Wave).

DOMINO THEORY

A popular theory in 1960s America, which held that one event could precipitate another in the same way that a row of dominoes will fall over one by one. This theory led the US to believe that the loss of Vietnam to communism would result in the loss of the whole of South-East Asia.

DOVER, GEORGE

A Hiver involved in a plot to cheat the Desert Inn, Las Vegas, to fund the construction of a gigantic Hive base beneath the desert near Area 51. (Dreamland).

DPs

When the alien ganglion is being rejected by its human host during the ART process, it emits a "distress pulse" (DP) on the Hive mindband. Totally inaudible to human ears, DPs are a call to arms for all Hive members within a five mile radius, putting the Artist under danger of almost immediate attack. Because of the danger of the DP, ART should always be performed in an isolated area to minimise the number of other Hive implantees in the area.

DREAMLAND

Otherwise known as Area 51. (Dreamland).

DULLES, ALLEN

The youngest of the two Dulles brothers, Allen Welsh Dulles was born in 1893. Following his studies at Princeton, Allen Dulles joined the US Diplomatic Service, serving in Berlin, Vienna, Bern, Paris and Istanbul. He quickly rose to become Chief of Division of Near Eastern Matters for the Department of State, but left the department in 1926 to spend almost twenty years working as a lawyer, before joining the US Office of Strategic Services in 1942.

Dulles became deputy director of the CIA in 1951 and within two years he had bagged the coveted position of Director. As Director of the CIA, it was Dulles who was responsible for the United States' involvement in the right wing coups that took place in 1953 in Iran and Guatemala. Dulles also involved the CIA in a series of missions in the USSR which were abruptly brought to a close when Francis Gary Powers' U-2 plane was shot down in Soviet airspace.

Dulles resigned from his position as Director of the CIA under a cloud when the disastrous Bay of Pigs affair of 1961 made a scapegoat of the agency. He spent the eight years until his death writing books about his experiences. (The Warren Omission).

DULLES, JOHN FOSTER

Born in 1888, John Foster Dulles began his political career at the tender age of nineteen, when he accompanied his diplomat grandfather to the Hague Conference of 1907. Twelve years later, in his capacity as a lawyer, Dulles was a legal adviser to the US delegation at the Versailles Peace Conference that settled the future of Europe at the end of World War One.

Dulles' conciliatory work continued when he was appointed consultant to the US delegation at the San Francisco UN conference of 1945. Not long after this, he was chosen by President Truman to negotiate the peace treaty with Japan at the end of World War Two.

It was Truman's successor, President Eisenhower, who made John Foster Dulles Secretary of State. Always a staunch anti-Communist, Dulles used his influence in this position to strengthen NATO against the Soviets with a series of pacts in Asia. For Dulles, communism was a moral issue. It was he who first coined the phrase "Better dead than red" and he also was the first to practise the political policy of "brinkmanship", pushing China and the USSR to the brink of war but not quite over it.

In April 1959, Dulles retired from the government through illness. He was awarded the Medal of Freedom and, when he died later that year, Washington DC's Dulles airport was named in his honour.

E.B.E INFECTION VECTOR
(See diagram below)

The E.B.E Infection Vector refers to the four-stage course of the hostile alien take-over of a human host.

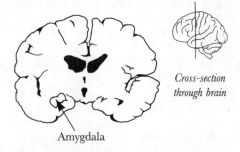

Cross-section through brain

Amygdala

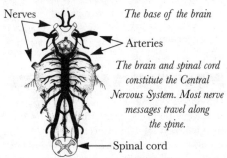

Nerves

The base of the brain

Arteries

The brain and spinal cord constitute the Central Nervous System. Most nerve messages travel along the spine.

Spinal cord

Alpha: The microbial stage. Immediately after implantation, new hosts will experience disorientation. They may hear voices and experience paranoia and extreme schizophrenic episodes. However, during this stage a host is not considered a successful candidate for ART.

Beta: The ganglion stage. Approximately twenty-four hours after implantation, a ganglion control site will have already been formed in the host's brain stem, specifically in the amygdala which controls the body's most basic functions. At this point, the ganglion begins to attack the host's Central Nervous System (CNS) by sending tendrils throughout. Most disturbingly, the host becomes aware of its predicament during this stage but is incapable of action. Several reported suicides have occurred during this stage. ARTs performed during the Beta phase have a success rate of approximately sixty percent.

Gamma: Nearly a year into the infection, the ganglion will have sent offshoots throughout the CNS in a process known as rooting, dominating the host completely. ART at this stage is practically impossible. In fact, the host can no longer be considered human and extermination is the preferred action upon discovery that a host is in the Gamma phase. Hosts in the Gamma phase are full-functioning Hive members. They have low-level telepathy skills and must be considered extremely dangerous.

Delta: A period of seven to ten years since implantation must lapse before the ganglion enters the Delta stage. The human host is now no more than a shell, whose Central Nervous System is composed almost entirely of ganglion tendrils. Deltas have longer range telepathic powers than Gammas. They can feel no pain, have an antipathy towards humanity and act without mercy towards humankind. During the New York City blackout of 1965, a Delta is reported to have burst free of its useless host shell and run amok.

E.B.E PROFILE

Developed by John Loengard during his work with Majestic in 1962, the EBE is a profile for the detection of "Extra-terrestrial Biological Entities". Loengard discovered that recent Hive implantees derived the majority of their emotional response information from non-verbal vocal cues, such as tone of voice rather than the actual words being spoken, and figured that this information could be used in detection. The EBE theory postulated that an implantee could be detected in the following way: the tester asks the suspected implantee nonsensical questions in a casual tone of voice. Because the implantee registers a normal tone of voice, he responds with normal answers, while a non-implantee recognises that the questions he is being asked are ridiculous. (The Awakening & The Enemy Within).

EDERMEYER, JOE

Journalist who went to Socorro to investigate Lonnie Zamora's claim that he had seen a UFO. (Hostile Convergence).

EISENHOWER, DWIGHT DAVID

Eisenhower was born on October 14th, 1890 in Denson, Texas. A graduate of West Point military academy, he enjoyed a successful career in the army which culminated with his appointment as Supreme Commander of the Allied Forces during the Second World War. As Supreme Commander, he was instrumental in the organisation of the D Day landings in Normandy which helped to bring about an end to the fighting in Europe.

Following the War, Eisenhower became Military Commander of NATO – a position he held until he was invited to run as the Republican Presidential Candidate in 1952. Eisenhower became the thirty-fourth president of the USA in 1953 after a sweeping electoral victory boosted by his popularity as a war hero, but Eisenhower was not as fanatical about defence as Truman had been. Instead he championed "modern republicanism" and emphasised the importance of fiscal conservatism. He sought to reduce taxes and decrease federal control of the economy. One of his greatest legacies to America was the Interstate highway system.

Internationally, Eisenhower's administration saw an end to the Korean war in 1953 and moves towards reconciliation with China and it was Eisenhower's Secretary of State, John Foster Dulles, who started to build up US forces against more likely trouble with the Soviets.

Under Dulles' guidance, Eisenhower extended Truman's NATO and ANZUS pact with the SEATO pact of 1954, while the Eisenhower Doctrine committed the United States to involvement in the Middle East, with a programme of economic and military aid to

Middle East governments who felt under threat from Soviet-inspired Arab nationalism. All seemed to be going well until the death of John Dulles, at which point, Eisenhower took a more active role in foreign policy himself. One of the last events of importance of Eisenhower's administration was the U-2 crisis of May 1st 1960, when an American U-2 jet was shot down in Soviet airspace. Eisenhower's last summit as President of the United States ended in disaster, with Krushchev demanding an apology that Eisenhower wouldn't give.

At the same time, the Soviets were leaping ahead of America in the race to get into space, and one of Eisenhower's last actions was to call for a crash program of federal assistance for the American space program.

ELWOOD, MRS.

Hive receptionist at the University of Wisconsin's Veterinary School who tried to grab back a child rescued by Sayers from one of the Hive's incubation cattle. (Inhuman Nature).

EPSTEIN, BRIAN

Manager of The Beatles, Epstein ignored Loengard's plea to tighten security around the Ed Sullivan Show performance. (Dark Day's Night).

FEDERAL BUREAU OF INVESTIGATION

More commonly known as the FBI, the Federal Bureau of Investigation is the investigative branch of the US Department of Justice. The FBI was founded by Attorney-General Charles J. Bonaparte in 1908 and was originally known more simply as the Bureau of Investigation. When J. Edgar Hoover was appointed as the bureau's director in 1924, he reorganised the bureau and gave it the power to investigate abuses of federal law. In the 1930's, the FBI was successful in keeping down the rising number of gangsters and during the Second World War, it was used to monitor the activities of Nazi sympathisers in the USA.

During the final years of Hoover's control of the FBI, its practices were brought into disrepute by its harassment of such radical activists as Martin Luther King, but, even today, the FBI plays a huge role in the enforcement of US law.

4 October 1957, USSR
The Soviet Union launched Sputnik One, the first ever artificial satellite, into orbit around the earth.

5 October 1957, South America
In South America, Antonio Villas Boas claimed that he had been abducted for the purposes of hybridisation experiments by his captors. This was the first report of an abduction involving a sexual element.

21 October 1957, Warwickshire, England
En route to RAF Gaydon in Warwickshire, Flight Officer D.W.Sweeney of RAF North Luffenham reported a near collision with a UFO. The report was confirmed by a radar reading at RAF Langtoft who knew of no other aircraft officially in that area at that time.

November 1957, USSR
The Soviet Union launched another satellite into space. This time the satellite had a passenger - astrodog Laika.

5 December 1957, United States
The United States tried to catch up with the Soviet Union in the space race with the launch of their satellite Vanguard. Vanguard didn't ever make it into orbit. The rocket's launch vehicle fell over and exploded two seconds after the fuse was ignited.

1957-58
International Geophysical Year or a massive cover-up for international UFO research?

31 January 1958, United States
A satellite launched from Cape Canaveral in Florida became the first United States satellite in orbit.

Inexplicable

19 April 1958, Lakenheath, England
Aircraft at RAF Lakenheath were scrambled to intercept a UFO. The mission was unsuccessful.

October 1958, United States/USSR/United Kingdom
Astronomers in America, the United Kingdom and the Soviet Union detected an object speeding towards the moon as a speed estimated to be faster than 25,000 m.p.h. Not only did they pick up the strange object on radar, they picked up its incomprehensible radio signals.

On The Record

18 Dec 1958, United States
The first atomic power plant was opened in Shippingport, Pennsylvania.

FLYING SAUCER

Nickname for the most commonly reported disc-shaped UFOs. The term "flying saucer" was coined in a 1947 newspaper report of a sighting by Idaho businessman Kenneth Arnold, who spotted a number of bright objects flying in formation over the Cascade Mountains in Washington State.

FLYIN' SAUCER SPECIAL

Split pea soup with ham, as served by Cassie, the Hive waitress, at Patrolman Lonnie Zamora's favourite Socorro diner. (Hostile Convergence).

FORCED CONSCIOUSNESS REPRESSOR

Otherwise known as an F.C.R, this is an oxygen-mask like device with a built-in inhaler that delivers a noxious gas to knock its wearer out. (The Warren Omission).

FORD, GERALD

A member of the House of Representatives in 1964, Gerald Ford was chosen to be a member of the Warren Commission which was formed to investigate JFK's death. Later, Gerald Ford was Republican vice-president during the Nixon administration and became President himself when Nixon resigned in 1974. (The Warren Omission).

FORRESTAL, JAMES V.

Secretary of the Navy and later Secretary of Defense in charge of the newly united US military forces, Forrestal was present at Roswell Army Air Base on the night of July 2, 1947. Forrestal suffered a mental breakdown in 1949, which led to his suicide in May of that year (see The Roswell Incident).

FRED

A furniture salesman from Moline, Illinois. Implanted by the Hive, Fred became one of their controlled gamblers at the Desert Inn in Las Vegas, raising funds to build a Hive headquarters in the desert beneath Area 51. (Dreamland).

FREEDOM SUMMER

A civil rights program initiated in Mississippi in the summer of 1964 by the Council of Federated Organisations. Thousands were recruited to participate in a drive to register as voters as many of Mississippi's 900,000 blacks as possible. Unfortunately, the initiative was quickly blighted by the disappearance of three civil rights workers, whose station wagon was found burned out fifteen miles north of Philadelphia.

A subsequent investigation revealed that the three men, two white and one black, had been put to death by members of the Ku Klux Klan.

FRIEND, MAJOR ROBERT J.

Head of Project Blue Book from 1958. (The Awakening).

FULLER, COLONEL PAUL

Pilot of the President's plane, Air Force One, Fuller was also a Hive implantee. When Loengard discovered this fact, he had Fuller taken off duty for the fly-past over President Kennedy's funeral, fearing a Hive plan to crash Air Force One into the assembled heads of state at the cemetery. (Moving Targets).

GALE, DR. JEFFREY

Dr. Gale diagnosed John Loengard as a paranoid schizophrenic when Loengard's father had him admitted to Fresno hospital for his own safety. (The Enemy Within).

GANGLION

An alien life form, resembling a crab or a lobster, which lives by taking over a host body, beginning by implanting itself in the host's amygdala before sending out tendrils throughout its host central nervous system. The ganglions together form The Hive. Evidence suggests that the Grays were a peaceful nation before they were taken over by the ganglions.

GANGLION CONTAINMENT DEVICE

A formidable head brace used by Majestic, which covers all the Hive implantee's orifices, mouth, nostrils, etc. so that the ganglion cannot escape from the host's body once that body starts to die. Since ganglions are usually evacuated alive, this prevents the possibility that the ganglion will try to find a new host in one of its captors, as happened when Jim Steele of Majestic was infected by the ganglion taken from Patient Zero. (Dark Day's Night).

GETTINGS, JACK

Floor manager of the Desert Inn Casino. (Dreamland).

GOULD, DAVID

An anthropology major from Queens College, Gould travelled to Mississippi on the first Freedom Summer bus to become a civil rights worker. Later he was one of three such workers to go missing in mysterious circumstances. (We Shall Overcome).

1959, Cuba
Led by their charismatic leader Fidel Castro, a group of guerrillas overthrew Fulgencio Batista, the island of Cuba's corrupt president. Batista had been supported by the American government but while American corporations had happily moved into Cuba and made a few people very rich, millions of ordinary Cubans were still starving. When Castro swept to power, he began to take steps to nationalise the factories and plantations that had been owned by the Americans and their puppets. While the ousted businessmen went to Washington to protest at his actions, Castro sat back and waited for the US to take action. Washington knew that something would have to be done, particularly since American investment was rapidly being replaced by Soviet aid.

1959, USSR
American Lee Harvey Oswald became a Soviet citizen.

1959, USSR
Soviet Air Defense personnel reported the appearance of UFOs which hovered and circled over Sverdlorsk, the headquarters of tactical missile organisation, for 24 hours.

GOULD, DR. HELEN

Dr. Gould worked as a hypnotist for NASA, ensuring the mental health of the astronauts of Midnight Wing before flights. (Mercury Rising).

GRABAR, FRED

On his first mission as a Majestic agent, Loengard used the pseudonym Fred Grabar when interviewing Elliot Grantham, owner of a field in which a Hive glyph had been found. (The Awakening).

PLANET EARTH
TIMELINE
Inexplicable

26 June 1959, Papua New Guinea Anglican priest William Gill collected signatures from 25 witnesses to support his report of a UFO sighting over his mission in Boianai. The next night, the UFOs returned and this time, Father Gill was able to watch the four occupants of what appeared to be the "mother ship" going about their business at the ship's deck while two smaller UFOs hovered nearby. When one of the humanoid figures looked down, Father Gill waved and was amazed to see the figure wave back at him. All four of the ship's occupants then climbed onto the top of the ship and waved for a few minutes before returning to their work. The ship allegedly hovered over Father Gill's mission for as long as an hour before the cloud cover became too dense for further observation of the visitors.

Over the course of that month, a further sixty sighting were made of strange craft.

PLANET EARTH
TIMELINE
Dark Skies

1 May 1960, United States Captain Frank Bach gave U2 pilot Gary Powers permission to overfly Soviet airspace in pursuit of an UFO. (The Awakening)

PLANET EARTH
TIMELINE
On The Record

10 May 1960, United States US Nuclear submarine Triton circled the globe underwater.

GRANTHAM, ELLIOT

An Idaho farmer. Owner of the field in which a Hive glyph was found imprinted into the corn. (Also see Patient Zero). (The Awakening).

GRAY, GORDON

Alleged to be one of the original twelve board members of Majestic-12, Gray was Assistant Secretary of the Army at the time of Majestic's inception. He later became Secretary of the Army and was appointed to be President Truman's Special Assistant on National Security Affairs.

GRAYS

Four bodies of non-terrestrial biology were recovered from the wreckage of their spacecraft outside Roswell, New Mexico in 1947. The creatures were reported to be between three-and-a-half and four feet tall with gray, leathery skin and large slanted black eyes. Three of these Grays were dead on arrival but a fourth was kept alive for a short time at Wright-Patterson Air Force Base. No communication was achieved.

In his book, *Aliens – The Final Answer*, David Barclay suggests another origin for the Grays. He cites the research of palaeontologist Dr. Dale A Russell, who extrapolated a biped creature similar to the Grays of popular ufology by applying the principles used to explain the evolution of mammals to the dinosaurs. Russell called his creature the "Stenonychosaurus". It had newt-like skin, a domed head with large eyes, while its nose and mouth were merely slits. The Stenonychosaurus also had claw like hands that would have been capable of manipulating advanced technology.

Barclay is convinced that the Extra-Terrestrials of popular ufology in fact originated from the same planet as the human race, but had to leave the planet when the crisis that wiped out the dinosaurs occurred. He cites the evidence of fossilised footprints found in prehistoric rock strata, which are too old to be the prints of Homo Sapiens, and the fact that most accounts of the Grays by abductees do not include references to breathing apparatus, suggesting that the Grays are fully adapted to the Earth's atmosphere. There are also accounts in which abductees claim to have been mated with Grays. This would be extremely dangerous for both the human being and the Grays if Grays and humans were really from different planets. An exchange of bodily fluids with a human would be fatal for a true extra-terrestrial creature since the human body contains toxic micro-organisms that can only be resisted with the protection of a human immune system developed over millennia of evolution.

HALLIGAN, DR. CHARLES

Majestic's chief physician.

HARGROVE, DONNA

Assistant to Hiver Ron Burnside, who ran pseudo-experiments in New York as part of the Hive's plan to make throwbacks commit suicide during The Beatles' appearance on the Ed Sullivan Show. (Dark Day's Night).

HELLER, NAT

A close friend of Loengard and Sayers from their days as students at UCLA. Nat was studying to be a marine biologist, but gave up his course to become a life-guard. Nevertheless, he used the knowledge he had already learned to discover a Hive-made synthetic micro-organism which was being pumped into the sea around Los Angeles. (The Last Wave).

HERTZOG, CARL

Majestic surgeon who invented the ART process as an alternative to surgically removing ganglions from their hosts, a process which almost always left the host dead. (The Awakening).

HILL, BETTY AND BARNEY

Betty and Barney Hill were driving home from a holiday in Canada on September 19, 1961, when they encountered a craft which Betty later described as a "flying pancake" hovering 200 feet ahead of them. When Barney went to investigate the curious apparition, he saw humanoid creatures inside the craft. They were wearing shiny black jackets and had malevolent slanted eyes.

Terrified by what he had seen, Barney was unable to move as the craft moved towards him, breaking free just in time to make it to the safety of his car and Betty before the craft landed. However, when Barney next looked at his watch, he saw that two hours had passed since he stopped the car to study the craft. Added to that was the fact that the Hills were 35 miles farther south than they should have been with

17 May 1960, France
The superpower summit in Paris came to an abrupt halt when the Soviet Union shot down a US U-2 plane which had overflown Soviet airspace. A deadlock occurred when Eisenhower refused to meet a demand from the Soviets to "apologise for past acts of aggression" and to punish those responsible for the U-2 entering Soviet airspace. At first, the State Department claimed that the plane, piloted by Gary Powers, was a weather plane.

May 1960, USSR
A U-2 plane, piloted by Francis Gary Powers, was shot down over the Soviet Union on May 1, 1960. Soviet Premier Krushchev reported that his country had shot down a spy plane and Powers was sentenced to ten years on spy charges.

However, it has since been speculated that Powers was actually in pursuit of a UFO and was given permission by Majestic-12 to overfly the Soviet Union. He was in fact shot down by the UFO but, to facilitate a cover-up, the United States was willing to let the Soviets claim that they had captured Powers on a spying mission. Powers was released in 1962 as part of an American/Soviet spy trade.

17 August 1960, USSR
In Moscow, U-2 pilot Gary Powers was sentenced to ten years in a Soviet prison and work farm for espionage. During his trial, Powers claimed that he had been following orders from the CIA when his plane strayed into Soviet skies.

24 September 1960, United States
The USS Enterprise, the biggest nuclear powered aircraft carrier, was launched into the James River. The Enterprise was 1,101 feet long, displaced 83,350 tonnes of water and had 8 reactors on board to power 4 propellers, at a cost of $365 million. The vast ship was able to circumnavigate the world 4 times without needing to be refuelled.

October 1960, United States
Fifty-two black people were arrested for the crime of entering a whites-only restaurant in Alabama. A Baptist minister, Dr. Martin Luther King, was subsequently convicted of the crime of "trespassing" and sentenced to four months' hard labour. Presidential candidate John F Kennedy intervened and King was released early.

9 November 1960, United States
John F Kennedy became the 35th President of the US with a majority of less than half of one percent or two votes per precinct. He was the second youngest President and the first ever Catholic to hold the office.

20 January 1961, Washington DC, United States
In his inaugural address, Kennedy told the nation that he was prepared to "pay any price, bear any burden, meet any hardship, support any friend, oppose any foe to assure the survival and success of liberty". Regarding relations with the USSR, he said "let us begin anew. Let us never negotiate out of fear. But let us never fear to negotiate." But at the beginning of Kennedy's term in office, the arms race was already escalating. The United States had 100 Atlas and Titan nuclear tipped rockets and there were plans for the deployment of 700 "Minuteman" missiles.

no recollection of how they had travelled that extra distance.

Thinking that they would become the laughing stock of the state, Betty and Barney Hill decided to keep their experience a secret until Barney was stricken with pains in his stomach and groin. His doctor told him that the pain sounded as though it had been caused by radiation.

Betty Hill meanwhile was suffering from a recurring nightmare, in which she encountered the ship and its strange inhabitants once again. Eventually, Betty and Barney took themselves to see a psychiatrist. That psychiatrist was Dr. Benjamin Simon, who investigated the couples' claims while they were under hypnosis.

The things that Betty and Barney remembered under hypnosis suggested that they had indeed been abducted by aliens, who must have subjected them to an invasive medical examination before returning them safely to their car. (The Awakening).

HILL, CLINT

Secret service agent with responsibility for the safekeeping of President Kennedy's body in transit between the scene of his assassination in Dallas and his final resting place in Washington. (Moving Targets).

HILLENKOETTER, ROSCOE H

Rear Admiral of the US Navy present at Roswell Army base on the night of the infamous Roswell Incident, Hillenkoetter later became the first Director of the CIA. Recently it has been alleged that Hillenkoetter was one of the original twelve directors of Majestic-12. Certainly he is known to have made public his conviction in the reality of UFOs. (Moving Targets).

THE HIVE

A term first coined by a Native American in reference to the alien's insect-like telepathic group consciousness. The Hive also describes an alien enclave within a town or city, where the alien life form tends to live in groups. At current rates of infection, the Hive will achieve "Singularity" by the year 2000.

HOOVER, J. EDGAR

Head of the FBI, Hoover's private life was the source of much speculation after it was revealed that he shared a house with another man, Clyde Tolson. (We Shall Overcome, The Warren Omission).

HUNSAKER, DR. JEROME

Head of the Department of Mechanical and Aeronautical Engineering at the Massachusetts Institute of Technology and Chairman of the National Advisory Committee for Aeronautics in 1947, Dr. Jerome Hunsaker is alleged to have been one of the twelve original directors of Majestic-12.

HYNEK, J. ALLEN

Head investigator for Project Blue Book, Hynek was sent to offer an explanation of the Socorro sighting. (Hostile Convergence).

HYPNAGOGIC STATE

One theory to explain the "alien abduction" experience suggests that it may be nothing but a dream . . . Psychologists making a study of sleep have defined a stage during which the body of the sleeper is effectively paralysed while the mind turns over the events of the day accompanied by the rapid eye movement (REM) that tells us when someone is dreaming. However, there are some people whose brains do not completely shut themselves off from the body during REM, and thus the sleeper receives messages that his or her body is actually participating in the events taking place during a dream. This is known as a "hypnagogic state".

One of the most commonly reported aspects of abduction experiences is of a heavy weight on the sleeper's chest, thought to be the weight of an alien pinning the sleeper down. During the Middle Ages this was interpreted as the weight of a demon. This sensation has been replicated in experimental conditions by inducing a hypnagogic state. In fact, when the state was induced in a UFO sceptic, she emerged from the state to report that she had been abducted herself. Of course, she had lain motionless in an observed laboratory during the time when she dreamed that she had been away.

There are also some people who dream so

PLANET EARTH TIMELINE
On The Record

21 January 1961, United States
President Kennedy's younger brother, Robert Kennedy, became Attorney General.

12 April 1961, USSR
The Soviets moved further ahead in the space race when Yuri Gagarin became the first man to orbit the earth.

24 April 1961, Cuba
President Kennedy's first initiative in the Cuban situation, named the "Bay of Pigs invasion", was a disaster.

11 May 1961, Vietnam
Kennedy approved the sending of 400 Special Forces soldiers and 100 military advisers to South Vietnam.

May 1961, United States
In Montgomery, Alabama, "The Freedom Riders", organised by James Farmer of the Congress of Racial Equality, made a stand against segregation.

5 May 1961, United States
Alan B Shephard Jr. became the first American in space. He was rocketed 115 miles high via an Army Redstone missile and was weightless for 5 minutes before drifting back to earth. Twenty days later, President Kennedy announced that "I believe this nation should commit itself to achieving the goal, before this decade is out, of landing a man on the moon and returning him safely to earth."

PLANET EARTH TIMELINE
Inexplicable

Summer 1961, USSR
Staff setting up surface to air missiles at Rybinsk near Moscow reported the appearance of a disc-shaped object flying at an altitude of 20,000 ft.

4 June 1961, Austria
President Kennedy and Soviet Premier Nikita Krushchev met at a summit in Vienna. During the course of the meeting the two men discussed the possibility of a Nuclear Test Ban Treaty and agreed that Laos should be neutral.

31 August 1961, USSR
A plane left the HQ of the tactical missile organisation at Sverdlorsk for Kurgan with seven passengers on board. Before it reached its destination the plane disappeared from the radar screen and was subsequently found in a clearing in the middle of dense forest, fully intact, but with no passengers on board. The Moscow Aviation Institute confirmed that they had tracked a UFO on radar at the time when the plane disappeared. They had also received incomprehensible radio signals.

19 September 1961, New Hampshire, United States
Driving back to their home in New Hampshire, Betty and Barney Hill noticed a bright light in the sky. Radar reports from nearby Pease Air Force Base also recorded something in the air at that time. Examining the light through binoculars, the Hills saw a structured object with flashing lights. Barney walked across a field for a closer view and saw people looking back at him from the craft. Frightened by what they had witnessed, Barney and Betty drove home, only to arrive two hours later than expected and unable to account for the missing time (a common phenomenon among abductees). Under regression hypnosis, the couple described being stopped by the UFO and taken aboard the saucer for medical examination.

vividly that they cannot accept that they were not in fact awake and actually experiencing the things they dreamed about.

HUGHES, HOWARD

An eccentric millionaire. Hughes was the heart-throb of Hollywood before he became a victim of obsessive compulsive disorder and became increasingly concerned with cleanliness, to the point that he would not go outside without wearing a mask for fear of breathing in germs. (Dreamland).

HUMPHREY, HUBERT

Senator for Minnesota. Later, Lyndon Johnson's vice-president.

JARVIS, EARL

The Sheriff of Fresno, who ordered Loengard's arrest after Loengard's father decided that his son was suffering from some kind of mental illness. (The Enemy Within).

JOHNSON, LYNDON

Older than Kennedy by almost a decade when he came to power in 1963, President Johnson was the thirty-sixth President of the USA. Born in 1908, Johnson served in the navy during World War Two and was elected to the Senate in 1948 as the representative for Texas in Congress. He became vice-president to John F. Kennedy in 1961.

When Kennedy was assassinated, Johnson was sworn in as President on the plane back from Dallas to Washington, with Jackie Kennedy at his side still wearing a suit splattered with her husband's blood. Johnson's first action as President was to push through the former President's welfare legislation, which included a number of Civil Rights Proposals, housing and urban development programmes, an increased education budget and medical care for the elderly. This undoubtedly increased Johnson's popularity and he swept to power again in a 1964 Presidential election with Hubert Humphrey as his second in command.

Though his administration saw a number of far-reaching social reforms, Johnson is most often remembered as the President who made a mess of the Vietnam War. By 1968, conscription and a high number of casualties had made him too unpopular to consider standing for re-election.

JULIET

A female Majestic agent with expertise in martial arts and Russian. Juliet made her entrance into Dark Skies mythology by kicking a freshly-bathed Loengard in the balls before stealing his towel and leaving him naked. (The Warren Omission).

KAUFMAN

A Majestic Cloaker. Kaufman almost managed to trap Sayers and Loengard, who were hiding in the basement of the University of Wisconsin with a human baby extracted from the stomach of a cow, but he was fooled by a nest of rats inside the baby's coat, giving Loengard and Sayers time to escape. (Inhuman Nature).

KENNEDY, JACKIE

Jackie Kennedy was born Jacqueline Lee Bouvier on July 28, 1929 to John Vernou Bouvier (otherwise known as "Black Jack") and his wife Janet Lee. Black Jack Bouvier was a charismatic stockbroker who made a fortune on the stockmarket and lost it again through gambling. Black Jack was also reputed to be a womanising drinker who was too drunk to give his own daughter away at her wedding to Senator John Kennedy in 1953.

Though she was an intelligent and educated woman, Jackie Kennedy quickly abandoned all career ambitions of her own to smooth the path to power for her husband. They had two children, Caroline and John Jr., but their marriage was not always a happy one. Historians believe that Jackie turned a blind eye to many of Kennedy's affairs (see Marilyn Monroe).

After Kennedy's death, Jackie went on to marry Greek shipping magnate Aristotle Onassis, which led to her reincarnation as "Jackie O". After his death, she returned to New York to work as a book editor until her retirement. She died of non-Hodgkin's lymphoma in 1995. (The Awakening, Moving Targets).

KENNEDY, JOHN FITZGERALD

America's first "television President", John F

Kennedy was also the first President to have been born in the 20th century. The second of nine children, Kennedy was born on May 29, 1917. Though his parents were second generation Irish, the world Kennedy came into was one of privilege and he was educated at private schools before studying at Princeton.

Having pulled strings to get a place in the Marines despite his poor health, Kennedy received a Purple Heart in 1943 for his heroic endeavour as skipper of Patrol Torpedo 109, which was based on the island of Tulagi in the South Pacific. PT 109 was hit by a Japanese destroyer, killing two of the sailors on board. Young JFK rescued several more, towing one of the injured men towards land with a rope held between his teeth.

His reputation as a war hero did JFK no harm when he began his political career in 1946. First he was elected as a Democratic member of the House of Representatives. Six years later he reached the Senate and narrowly missed the vice-presidency in 1956.

Kennedy rose to power in 1960 through a Presidential election fought against Richard "Tricky Dicky" Nixon. He became the youngest ever President and the first Catholic to hold the role by the narrowest margin possible. He won by 34,227,096 votes to Nixon's 34,106,646. That margin represented a win by less than two votes per precinct or less than half of one percent of the total polled.

Like Eisenhower before him, Kennedy had been a "Cold Warrior" in his election campaign, staying quiet on civil rights issues because he didn't wish to alienate the Southern Democrats. In fact, he had made a few political enemies by appearing to duck the issue of McCarthyism during his political career. Once in power however, he took President Roosevelt's campaign as his model, promising America a "New frontier" to "get this country moving again".

Kennedy strongly believed that wise policy emerged from debate and he surrounded himself with some of the finest minds around. He was advised primarily by Clark Clifford, a Washington lawyer, and Richard Neustadt, a Columbia political scientist. However, his brilliant advisers didn't prevent Kennedy from making a disastrous mistake with the Bay of

3 October 1961, Washington DC, United States Having recently graduated from UCLA, John Loengard moved to Washington to take up a job in the office of Congressman Charles Pratt. Loengard was accompanied by his girlfriend Kimberley Sayers.

9 November 1961, United States At Edwards Air Force Base in California, Major Robert White broke the world speed record in an X15 jet. He reached 4070 mph at a height of 100,000ft. The aircraft suffered a cracked windscreen but the pilot was unhurt.

11 December 1961, New Hampshire, United States As part of his investigation of Project Blue Book, Loengard paid a visit on Betty and Barney Hill, the couple who claimed to have been abducted from their car. Later that night, Loengard had his first encounter with Captain Bach and Majestic.

10 February 1962, United States U2 pilot Gary Powers was returned to the US in exchange for the freedom of Russian spy Rudolph Abel.

Pigs Affair, or keep him from getting increasingly involved with the unpopular cause of Vietnam. In fact, a Gallup poll taken on 10th November 1963, twelve days before JFK's assassination, showed that only 59% of the American people approved of his policies – an all-time low in JFK's popularity stakes.

Three days after his death by assassination in November 1963 however, the picture was very different. A poll taken then by the National Opinion Research Centre at the University of Chicago showing that 80% of the American people rated John F Kennedy as an above average President. In fact 50% rated him as one of the best ever.

In 1967, Walt Lippman summed up America's relationship with John F Kennedy by saying that: "A passionate multitude all over the world believed him to have been the herald of better things in dangerous and difficult times."

When President Lyndon Johnson came to power two hours after Kennedy's death, his difficult times were just beginning. (The Awakening, Moving Targets).

KENNEDY, ROBERT F

JFK's younger brother Bobby Kennedy, born in 1925, master-minded the 1960 election campaign. When JFK became President, Bobby became his Attorney-General, an appointment which caused much controversy due to Bobby's lack of experience. JFK's comment on the matter was "I don't see what's wrong with giving Bobby a little experience before he starts to practice law."

Despite his inexperience, Bobby went on to play a very important role in the Kennedy administration, possibly even averting a sticky ending to the Cuban Missile Crisis with his response to Krushchev's provocation, which was far more level-headed than his brother's.

After JFK's assassination, Bobby Kennedy set his sights on continuing the Kennedy dynasty by becoming President himself. He was a candidate for the Democratic nomination in the 1968 Presidential election, but just as his support reached its peak, Bobby, like his brother before him, fell at the hands of an assassin.

Robert Kennedy was killed by Sirhan Bishara "Sol" Sirhan, a native of Jordan, on 4th June 1968, the first anniversary of the Israeli-Arab six-day war. Sirhan's motive was that Kennedy had expressed his support for the Israelis. Ironically, Robert Kennedy had once commented, shortly after the death of his brother, that "an assassin never changed the course of history".

KGB

The Soviet equivalent of the CIA, the KGB (an abbreviation of the Russian for Committee of State Security), was formed in 1953, as a vehicle for the regulation of external espionage and internal counter-intelligence.

KINCAID, MAX

Justice agent assigned to protect Sayers and Loengard while they awaited Loengard's appearance before the Warren Commission. (The Warren Omission).

KING, MARTIN LUTHER JR.

Born in Atlanta, Georgia on January 15, 1929, Martin Luther King Jr. is arguably the most famous civil rights activist of all time.

Luther King came from a family of Baptist ministers, but decided against that career path as he was growing up because he was committed to the civil rights cause and felt that the church was not the right place to air civil rights issues. King's mind was changed while studying as an undergraduate at Morehouse College. There he met a professor who persuaded him that there was no better place to preach civil rights than from the pulpit and King continued his education at Crozer Theological Seminary, graduating from there at the top of his class.

Having finished off his education in Boston, King first became pastor of the Dexter Avenue Baptist Church in Montgomery, Alabama. There he formed the Montgomery Improvement Association and became involved in his first high profile battle when he took up the case of Rosa Parks. Ms. Parks, a black woman, had been arrested and fined for refusing to give up her seat on a bus to a white man. With the MIA, King encouraged blacks to boycott the bus company and the economic pressure forced the local government to change the law under which Rosa Parks had been charged.

From his Montgomery triumph, King went on to co-found the Southern Christian Leadership Conference and became the Pastor of Ebenezer Baptist Church. In 1963, he led protests in Birmingham, Alabama and was arrested for his troubles. It was at this time that King wrote his famous "Letter from Birmingham Jail", in which he urged his followers that non-

violence should be the key note of their campaign. His theme was taken up by college students, who organised sit-ins at their colleges, and by the Congress of Racial Equality who organised "freedom rides" in honour of Rosa Parks.

Later in 1963, King led the "March on Washington Campaign". Originated by Philip Randolph of the Brotherhood of Sleeping Car Porters, the March on Washington was originally intended to be a protest about jobs and working conditions. With Martin Luther King Jr. at the forefront however, it soon became a march about freedom. More than 250,000 people marched alongside King to the Lincoln Memorial, which commemorates Lincoln's Emancipation Proclamation, the bill which gave freedom to Negro slaves 100 years before King's anniversary march on 28th August 1963.

Of the 250,000 marchers, at least a third were white. Each marcher wore a 25 cent badge displaying a black hand clasping a white hand. As they marched, they sang "We shall overcome" and there was no hint of violence throughout the day. Amongst the audience who gathered to listen to King were famous musicians Bob Dylan, Joan Baez, and Peter, Paul and Mary. Josephine Baker was there too, as was baseball star Jackie Robinson . . . and Malcolm X, who would denigrate King's policy of non-violence to anyone who would listen to him.

King was the last speaker of the day, telling the crowd that he was "happy to join with you today in what will go down in history as the greatest demonstration for freedom in the history of our nation." He talked about the "great beacon light of hope" that was Lincoln's Emancipation Proclamation, but seemed disappointed by the Kennedy administration which, he said, had "given the Negro people a bad check; a check which has come back marked 'insufficient funds',," though King "refused to believe that the bank of justice is bankrupt". King had in fact asked President Kennedy to issue a "Second Emancipation Proclamation" to no avail, leading King to conclude that Kennedy was "fumbling on the New Frontier" and that the government was "proudly professing the principles of democracy" then "practising the very antithesis of those principles" . On that day in Washington, King told the crowd

PLANET EARTH TIMELINE

Dark Skies

17 February 1962, Washington DC, United States
Loengard challenged Captain Bach about Majestic and found himself getting more than the truth. Bach took Loengard into Majestic HQ and showed him the cadaver of a Gray. Having seen this, Loengard had no choice but to become a Majestic agent himself.

PLANET EARTH TIMELINE

On The Record

20 February 1962, United States
John H Glenn Jr. made an orbital flight three times around the earth. His flight was not without problems however. The jet designed to maintain the ship's orientation malfunctioned and panic ensued when instruments at ground stations seemed to indicate that the heat shield to protect Glenn on re-entry had become detached from the main body of the craft. Fortunately John landed safely near Grand Turk Island in the Bahamas, 700 miles south of Cape Canaveral.

22 March 1962, Vietnam
US troops began Operation Sunrise to transfer loyal South Vietnamese from Communist infiltrated areas of Vietnam.

17 May 1962, Laos
Forces were deployed in Laos in a move which President Kennedy claimed as an "act of diplomacy".

11 July 1962, Andover, Maine, United States
The Telstar Communications Satellite was rocketed into orbit, to beam television broadcasts all over America.

that "we have come to this hallowed spot to remind America (that) now is the time to rise from the dark and desolate valley of segregation to the sunlit path of racial justice".

Concluding his speech that day, King uttered the words which have come to symbolise him and all that he stood for, "I have a dream . . ."

President Kennedy never did issue a Second Emancipation Proclamation and like Kennedy, Martin Luther King Jr. met an untimely end. King was shot dead while standing on the balcony of a hotel room in Memphis, Tennessee. The day before he had appeared at a rally in support of striking sanitation workers. Martin Luther King Jr. was buried in the South View Cemetery in Atlanta, though his body was later moved to the Martin Luther King Jr. Centre for Non-violent Social Change. (We Shall Overcome).

KISSINGER, HENRY ALFRED

Henry Kissinger was a government consultant on defence between 1955 and 1968. In 1969, Kissinger was appointed as head of the National Security council by President Nixon, a role in which he was responsible for the improvement of relations between the USSR and the USA resulting in the Strategic Arms Limitation Treaty (SALT). Kissinger can also claim credit for the final resolution of the Vietnam War.

KOREAN WAR

In 1948 Korea was split into a communist north and a democratic south. War broke out in 1950, when the North Koreans launched a surprise attack on the South. The South Koreans, with the help of US forces under General MacArthur, launched a counter-offensive and took two months to push the North Koreans back over the border. But by now the Chinese had entered the conflict on the side of North Korea, starting in earnest a war which lasted until the 27th July 1953, when an armistice signed at Panmunjom set the new boundary between North and South Korea at a battle line close to the original boundary of 1948.

KRUSHCHEV, NIKITA SERGEYIVICH

Kennedy's Soviet counterpart, Nikita Krushchev, born in 1894, rose to power as the First Secretary of the Communist Party upon the death of Stalin in 1953. Krushchev was devoted to improving the agriculture of the

Soviet Union and introduced widespread reforms of the regional economic administration and law enforcement agencies which had become so corrupt under Stalin. Outside the Soviet Union, Krushchev crushed anti-Soviet revolutions in Poland and Hungary. He had a bitter feud with Mao Tse Tung of China which nearly resulted in a Sino-Soviet war but his policy towards the West was one of "peaceful co-existence". However, even this was threatened in 1962, when the Soviets and the US came close to nuclear war over the Cuban Missile Crisis.

As a result of his handling of the Cuban and other foreign crises, Krushchev was forcibly removed from his office as Soviet premier in 1964.

KU KLUX KLAN

A secret society founded in Southern USA after the American Civil War which espoused white supremacy. The Ku Klux Klan is famous for its uniform of white robes with pointed hoods that cover all but the wearer's eyes. Also known as the KKK, this bigoted group of people spread fear amongst the black population of America and was responsible for the deaths of nearly two thousand people by lynching.

At the height of its hate campaign, the KKK boasted some four million members, including federal and state officials. Though it has declined considerably, it still exists amongst the more backward-thinking white communities in some southern states of the USA. (We Shall Overcome).

THE LADY DIES YOUNG

A 1938 Hollywood movie starring Bette Davis. When Loengard and Sayers are taken to see eccentric billionaire Howard Hughes, he is watching this film and tells them how he once planned to make a remake staring Jane Russell during his days at Republic. (Dreamland).

LANE, MARNIE

Marnie Lane met Sayers and Loengard in New York, when she attended a Hive-run experiment to try to earn enough money to see The Beatles on the Ed Sullivan Show. When the advertisements she was viewing as part of the experiment caused her to react by feeling ill, she left the

experiment, followed by Sayers, who got Marnie to confide in her. By listening to the contents of a recurring dream which Marnie had been having, Sayers worked out that Marnie was an abduction throwback and deduced that the experiment must therefore have been set up to affect throwbacks in some way. Marnie eventually got to see The Beatles in concert from the side of the stage after Loengard prevented her from throwing herself from the auditorium circle when she heard a song containing a Hive stimulus. (Dark Day's Night).

LAOS

Occupied by the Japanese during World War Two, the small south east Asian country of Laos fell under the communist influence of Pathet Lao in the mid 1950s. Laos became an important piece of territory in terms of American foreign policy as it represented another communist "domino" in south-east Asia, that could add strength to the North Vietnamese campaign to unite Vietnam as a communist state.

LEWIS, CLAYTON

A white supremacist from Meridian, Mississippi, Lewis was forced to work alongside his black nemesis, Langston Poole, after being implanted by the Hive. Lewis was subsequently ART-d by Sayers and Loengard, despite seeming unable to give up his prejudices to see who the "real enemy" was. Though Lewis never renounced his beliefs, Sayers was certain that it was he who donated the money to rebuild Langston Poole's church after it was burned to the ground by Majestic. (We Shall Overcome).

LILY

A cow belonging to Farmer Kester Boehm of Monticello, Wisconsin. Following an investigation into her ill-health by trainee vet Mark Waring, Lily was found to have a curious growth in her third stomach, or rumen. When the growth was removed, it was discovered to contain a perfect boy-child, of approximately two years of age. This discovery led Loengard and Sayers to believe that the Hive might be incubating human children in cows to be used as hosts later on. (Inhuman Nature).

LINCOLN, EVELYN

Personal assistant to President Kennedy. (Moving Targets).

LOENGARD, DICK

Father of John Loengard, Dick Loengard was sceptical of his son's involvement with Dark Skies until he discovered that his elder son Ray had been implanted by the Hive. Dick Loengard had John briefly incarcerated in hospital, thinking that he might be suffering from a mental illness. (The Enemy Within).

LOENGARD, JO

John Loengard's mother. (The Enemy Within).

LOENGARD, JOHN

John Loengard, ex-Majestic agent and founder member of the Dark Skies movement. (See extended character profile).

LOENGARD, LUCY

John Loengard's younger sister. (The Enemy Within).

LOENGARD, RAY

Loengard's elder brother Ray was implanted with a ganglion during a camping trip in the forest near his home. As a child, Ray almost drowned in a river near his home but was rescued by John, the better swimmer. Jim Steele tried to use Ray as an assassin, asking him to kill his brother, but Ray's memories of his childhood debt to John overrode the Hive's instruction and instead he laid down his life for his brother's. (The Enemy Within).

LOMILLER, JOHN

Loengard used the pseudonym John Lomiller while posing as an anthropology student investigating the phenomenon of the floating rocks in Chiliwack, Alaska. (Ancient Future).

MACARTHUR, GENERAL DOUGLAS

General MacArthur was the US Army chief of staff between 1930 and 1935. He retired from the army in 1937 but was called out of retirement by President Roosevelt during the Second World War to strengthen Allied defences in the Philippines, subsequently becoming the commander of the Allied occupation forces.

Later, as the UN commander in the Korean War, MacArthur took the US to the brink of atomic war and, as a result, was dismissed by President Truman in 1951. MacArthur then tried and failed to obtain a nomination for the Presidential election in 1952. He died in 1964.

MCCARTHY, JOSEPH

McCarthy was a Republican Senator for Wisconsin when he launched his campaign claiming the existence of a communist plot to infiltrate the US government in the early 1950s. A subsequent investigation by Millard Tydings seemed to indicate that there was no such plot, but McCarthy continued to make allegations against members of the government, the military and even figures in the arts, such as playwright Arthur Miller. The result was a "witch-hunt", during which McCarthy conducted a series of televised hearings where many public figures were accused of scandalous and treacherous behaviour and had their reputations ruined. Eventually, McCarthy was denounced by President Eisenhower and was censured by the Senate for his troubles.

MCCLOY

US citizen present at the hearing of the Warren Commission into the assassination of JFK. (The Warren Omission).

MAJESTIC-12

Also known as MJ-12 (12 being a reference to the dozen directors who historically set policy), Majestic was officially formed in 1947 in response to the Roswell Incident. Operating in the utmost secrecy, MJ-12 was responsible only to the President, although even that command link was abandoned under the leadership of Lt. Frank Bach in 1961. The organisation was severely compromised by alien infiltration in 1965.

To this day, MJ-12 remains the subject of intense speculation by UFO enthusiasts, while its existence is totally denied by the United States government. In 1984, the case was reopened when Hollywood producer Jaime Shandera received an anonymous parcel containing photographs of documents pertaining to Majestic-12. The first was a memo from President Truman, authorising the implementation of "Operation Majestic Twelve". The second was a briefing paper from Rear Admiral Roscoe Hillenkoetter to President-elect Dwight Eisenhower, which listed the names of the twelve original directors. The authenticity of these documents has not been satisfactorily proved but the existence of Majestic-12 has also been confirmed by word of mouth reports from top military personnel of the 1940s and 1950s. Certainly, there are references to a number of small "top secret" groups set up to investigate UFOs in military correspondence about the time that Majestic-12 is alleged to have been formed.

MALCOLM X

Born in Omaha, Nebraska on May 19, 1925, Malcolm X went through many incarnations until he became the ideological leader we remember him as today.

The son of a Baptist preacher and a housewife from Grenada, Malcolm was born into a family which knew more than most the importance of civil rights. By the age of four, Malcolm had seen his home burned down by racists, and when his family finally gave up on Omaha and left the town, Malcolm's father was killed in a lynch mob attack in Michigan. Later at school, Malcolm was discouraged from becoming a lawyer by a teacher who advised him that a "nigger" should become a labourer instead.

Little wonder then that Malcolm seemed to go off the rails. In 1946 he was sentenced to ten years in prison for dealing drugs. But it was while he was in prison that he underwent a transformation. He discovered Islam and on his release he joined the Nation of Islam with the intention of using the organisation as a platform for spreading the word about black radicalism. While with the NOI he set up a newspaper called *Muhammad Speaks* which became the radical black newspaper of the sixties and first became known as Malcolm X (with the X standing for the African tribe of his ancestors that he had never known).

However, in 1964, Malcolm X broke with the Nation of Islam to form the Organisation

5 August 1962, United States Attorney-General Robert Kennedy kept a rendezvous with his lover, Marilyn Monroe.

5 August 1962, United States Movie star Marilyn Monroe was found dead in her bed in Hollywood, California. Suicide was given as the official cause of death.

20 October 1962 Majestic agent Popejoy was killed by a chimpanzee which had been implanted with an alien ganglion.

21 October 1962
Kim Sayers was abducted from her bedroom by the Grays. Other abductees on that night included Gary Augatreux and Ty Yount, who were astronauts on the "unmanned" Gemini mission launched on that day.

28 October 1962, Cuba
The Cuban Missile Crisis. A week of incredible tension during which America went to the brink of nuclear war with the Soviet Union over Cuba. A UN aide reported this week as the "first real, direct confrontation between the super powers". Krushchev was eventually forced to withdraw missiles from Cuba and Cuba saw America's actions as a declaration of war. In response Kennedy told his nation, "the cost of freedom is always high, but Americans have always paid it."

of Afro American Unity, the political arm of Muslim Mosque Inc. He also broke with the Nation of Islam's interpretation of the religion

18 December 1962,
Nassau, The
Bahamas
The Anglo-
American agree-
ment on nuclear
collaboration known as the Nassau
Agreement was signed.

10 April 1963, Boston, United States
The Nuclear submarine Thresher sank
off the coast not far from Boston.
Admiral George Anderson said that he
had "no good theory to explain the
disaster."

13 May 1963, Alabama, United States
Civil rights activist Martin Luther
King was freed from jail in
Birmingham, Alabama.

11 June 1963, Alabama, United States
Racial Integration finally came to
Birmingham, Alabama.

28 August 1963, Washington DC, United
States
Martin Luther King Jr. led the
250,000 people in the March on
Washington. At the end of a day of
venerable speakers, King delivered his
famous "I have a dream" speech.

30 August 1963, United States/USSR
A direct hotline was established
between the White House in Washington
DC and the Kremlin in Moscow to ease
the path of superpower communications.

10 October 1963, Switzerland
The USA, the Soviet Union and Britain
signed the Limited Nuclear Test Ban
Treaty.

---

and made a pilgrimage to Mecca, whereupon he took the name "El-Hajj Malik El Shabazz". Tensions had been growing between Malcolm X and the NOI for some time, culminating when he was suspended for 90 days in 1964 following a tactless comment after Kennedy's assassination that the atrocity represented "The chickens coming home to roost".

In January 1965, Malcolm X pronounced

that "It is incorrect to classify the revolt of the Negro as simply a racial conflict of Black against White or as a purely American problem. Rather we are today seeing a global rebellion of oppressed against the oppressor, the exploited against the exploiter." The lasting impact of Malcolm X is due largely to how he represented the radical black tradition in confronting the white establishment. He exploited the mainstream media, appearing on both radio and TV.

After a long period of demeaning his contemporary Martin Luther King Jr's policy of non-violence in the struggle for equality, Malcolm X was assassinated by three gunmen at a rally in the Audubon Ballroom, Harlem in February 1965. (We Shall Overcome).

MAO TSE-TUNG

Leader of the Chinese Communist Party (1934 -1976) and chairman of the People's Republic of China.

MARCEL, JESSE

Present at Roswell Air Force base on the night of the infamous Roswell Incident, Marcel later became involved with the Dark Skies movement when President Kennedy entrusted him with a valuable artefact taken from Roswell just hours before his assassination. (The Awakening, Moving Targets, Hostile Convergence).

Major Jesse Marcel is the real name of the intelligence officer of the 509th Bomb Group, the world's first atomic bomb unit, which was based at the Roswell Army Air Field. In the 1970's Marcel spoke to a journalist about the night of the Roswell Incident, confirming that the material recovered that night did not look like the remains of a weather balloon to him.

MARSHALL PLAN

The Marshall Plan, passed by Congress in 1948, was designed to offer economic assistance to European states recovering from the terrible devastation of World War II. All the European nations were invited to partake of the aid offered by the USA but the Soviet Union declined and encouraged its Eastern European satellites to also ignore the helping hand. Therefore, essentially the Marshall Plan came to represent an American attempt to bribe

Europe to turn its back on the temptations of communism.

MENDEL, ANDREW

A social worker from New York. Andrew was just twenty-four when he went missing near Philadelphia, Mississippi, believed murdered for his work on civil rights. (We Shall Overcome).

MENZEL, DONALD

Director of the Harvard College Observatory, Dr. Donald Menzel wrote a number of publications dismissing UFOs during the 1950s, despite the fact that he is alleged to be one of the twelve original directors of Majestic-12.

M.I.B.

Early MJ-12 protocol called for its field agents to dress "uniformly and unobtrusively", and M.I.B. stands for the "Men-In-Black", spotted at crime scenes throughout the 50's and 60's, who were considered untouchable by the FBI and the CIA. Eventually the Men In Black abandoned their smart suits for ordinary street clothes to provide more realistic cover.

MITTERMEYER, ERNST

Majestic's geologist, assigned to investigate the floating rocks in Chiliwack, Alaska. (Ancient Future).

THE MONKEY FILM

The infamous Monkey Film captured a Rhesus monkey, artificially implanted with ganglion tissue, opening his cage door by operating a numerically sophisticated lock mechanism. Later in the film, the same monkey was seen attacking its captors, actually firing a small revolver during the attack.

Doctor Carl Hertzog leaked the only existing copy of the Monkey Film to a journalist, who in turn urged John Loengard to present the film to the Warren Commission.

The Monkey Film was scheduled to be broadcast as part of a network news exposé in November of 1965. To prevent this, a Hive spacecraft was used to cause an overload in the north-east's electrical system, resulting in the New York black-out.

The Monkey Film is no longer in existence. (The Awakening).

MONROE, MARILYN

Born plain old Norma Jean Mortenson (also known as Baker) on June 1st, 1926 in Los Angeles, Marilyn Monroe was the daughter of a largely absent father and a mother who worked as a film-cutter at RKO pictures. Sadly, even little Norma Jean's mother deserted her eventually and she spent her childhood drifting between orphanages and foster homes before she became a model.

Marilyn Monroe's first big break came in 1946 when she was signed to Twentieth Century Fox for the princely sum of $125 a week. Twentieth Century Fox had plenty of pretty girls on similar contracts, but Marilyn proved that she was special and was soon the most popular face on garage walls all over America. Truly recognised as a star when she acted in *The Seven Year Itch* in 1954, Monroe also made a habit of marrying famous men. Her second husband was top baseball player Joe Di Maggio; her third husband, the acclaimed playwright Arthur Miller.

Though her stage image was that of a dizzy blonde, Monroe's interests ranged far wider than what dress she should wear next. She was also interested in politics and was attracted to the Kennedy brothers, John and Robert, because in her eyes they represented the abused and the abandoned, a group amongst whom she counted herself.

Monroe may have met the Kennedys as early as 1951 in the company of her agent, Charles Feldman, who was a Kennedy family friend. Just before John Kennedy's inauguration, she is rumoured to have told a friend about her "date with the next president of the United States" and on his first birthday as President she performed "Happy Birthday" for him at Madison Square Gardens in her own inimitably breathless way.

Towards the end of Monroe's life, rumours that she was having affairs with both the Kennedy brothers abounded. Certainly, both John and Robert were interested in the Hollywood scene, since their father Joe had been involved in movie finance, and it is proba-

PLANET EARTH TIMELINE

Inexplicable

17 October 1963, Falkville, Alabama, United States

Police chief Jeff Greenshaw responded to the call of a young woman who said that she had seen a UFO land in a field just outside town. When Greenshaw arrived at the scene to investigate, he saw a figure standing in the middle of a dirt track. The figure was wearing a protective silvery suit, and antennae seemed to sprout from its head. Greenshaw managed to shoot four pictures of the figure before it disappeared. Though many people had reported odd lights over Alabama that night, Greenshaw was subsequently relieved of his duties as a police officer.

PLANET EARTH TIMELINE

On The Record

2 November 1963, Vietnam

The South Vietnamese premier, Ngo Dinh Diem, was assassinated in Saigon.

ble that Monroe saw an alliance with the Kennedys as completing the ambitious, intellectual profile she wanted to show the world.

Things seem to have gone sour however. As speculation about her sexual involvement with the Kennedy boys mounted, Monroe became convinced that her phones were being tapped. Then she complained that the Kennedys had cut her dead.

Marilyn was found dead in her bed in 1962. The official cause of death was suicide. However, George Cukor called her demise "a nasty business". He claimed it was the result of "Her worst rejection. Power and money. In the end she was too innocent." Power and money being, it seems, a clear reference to the Kennedy clan.

Monroe's physician, Dr. Greenson, fiercely denied rumours that Monroe had been involved in an affair with either the President or the Attorney General, but said that during his last telephone conversation with Monroe she had sounded "drugged and depressed" because her meeting with one of the "very important people" she had been seeing had been called off. Greenson also suggested to Dr. Robert Litman of the suicide investigation squad that Monroe found it "gratifying to have a close relationship with extremely important men in government . . . a sexual relationship . . . at the highest level." Another clear reference to the Kennedys.

Was Monroe depressed enough by the break-up of her relationship with the Kennedy men to kill herself? Perhaps one of the most telling comments on the affair came from a Hollywood agent who, upon being told of the suicide, is reputed to have cried "It can't be, it can't be. She had three deals going." (The Warren Omission).

MONTAGUE, GENERAL ROBERT

General Robert Montague was commander of the Atomic Energy Commission installation at Sandia Base, Albuquerque, New Mexico, when he is alleged to have been recruited to the first board of directors of Majestic-12.

MORRISON, JIM

Jim Morrison, best known as the lead singer of The Doors, was born on December 8th 1943 in Melbourne, Florida. He was the son of Steve Morrison, a US navy recruit, who worked as an instructor on the atomic weapons program before rising through the ranks to become captain of the USS Bon Homme.

It was on one of the Morrison family's many journeys between Steve's military postings that young Jim Morrison had what he described as "the most important moment of his life". On the road from Santa Fe, the Morrison family passed an overturned truck. Getting out to investigate the accident, Steve Morrison found that the truck had been carrying a family of Pueblo Indians who were now dying of their injuries by the side of the road. Steve sent word that an ambulance was needed but it was too late to save one of the victims. Young Jim was hysterical and claimed from that moment on that, as his father drove away from the scene of the accident, the spirit of a dying Indian passed into Jim Morrison's body.

Little wonder then that Jim grew up to seem so "different" from the other kids. At school he was an avid reader, devouring the likes of German philosopher Friedrich Nietzsche and French poets Charles Baudelaire and Arthur Rimbaud. Later Morrison started to write poetry of his own, many of his verses having the recurring themes of water and death.

As a young adult, Morrison dropped out of Florida State University against his parents' wishes and enrolled as a cinematography student at UCLA. There he was privileged enough to be taught by such directors as Stanley Kramer, Jean Renoir and Josef Von Sternberg. Among Jim's fellow students was a young Francis Ford Coppola (director of *Dracula*) who would later use Morrison's seminal work "The End" on the soundtrack of his film *Apocalypse Now*. But unlike Coppola, Jim was not an ideal film student.

At the end of the first year of the cinematography course, the students were required to present a short film of their work. Jim's friend, Phil Oleno, had circumvented this requirement by appearing in a film instead. Oleno had taken part in a sequence shot by the Psychology Department which was supposed to be a scientific study of the postures assumed during love-making. The film was supposed to be top secret but somehow Morrison managed to get hold of some outtakes of Oleno and his fellow subject, a young woman, romping in the nude in the name of science and set the embarrassing footage to Ravel's Bolero. When Morrison presented this "film" at his end of term assessment, his tutors were furious. For his efforts they awarded him the lowest possible grade and assigned him to a class for problem students.

Morrison's diaries from his years at UCLA make interesting reading. Frequently peppered with images of sex, violence and death, the diaries also refer to President Kennedy being assassinated with the sniper's "injurious vision" and talk of Lee Harvey Oswald as having found a haven "devoured in the warm dark silent maw of the physical theatre."

Morrison eventually quit film school just two weeks before he was due to finish classes. His exit came two days after a screening at which

PLANET EARTH TIMELINE

On The Record

22 November 1963, Dallas, Texas, United States President John F Kennedy was assassinated during an official visit to Dallas, Texas. Less than 2 hours after Kennedy's death, President Lyndon Johnson was sworn in as the 36th president aboard Air Force One. Jackie Kennedy stood alongside him, still wearing a pink suit splattered with her husband's blood.

Security forces arrested Lee Harvey Oswald for the crime. The twenty-four year old former marine, who had become a Soviet citizen in 1959, was known to be active in the Fair Play for Cuba Committee. He was believed to have killed Kennedy with three shots from the sixth floor of the Texas School Book Depository on Elm Street, where he had been employed as a clerk. The first bullet hit Kennedy in the back, a second in the back of his head. Texan Governor John B Connally who was travelling in the President's car was also wounded. Ironically, the President had asked for the protective bubble that usually covered his car to be left off that day, since the weather was so fine.

The president was rushed to the Parkland Memorial Hospital but was pronounced dead at one o'clock. A victim of his own "dangerous and untidy world".

he was awarded a "D" for his latest cinematographic efforts. That was the end of his film career. Morrison went on to form The Doors with Ray Manzarek, Roddie Krieger and John Densmore. Their name was taken either from a poem by William Blake which said that "There are things that are known and things that are unknown: in between are The Doors," or maybe from Aldous Huxley's work describing his experiences on mescaline which said that "all the other chemical Doors in the Wall are labelled Dope." Whichever source you believe tells you whether Jim

24 November 1963, Dallas, Texas, United States
Kennedy assassination suspect Lee Harvey Oswald was himself killed by Jack Ruby, the owner of a Dallas night-club, who shot Oswald in the stomach at close range.

25 November 1963, Washington DC, United States
Kennedy was buried at Arlington National Cemetery following a mass at St. Matthew's Roman Catholic Cathedral in Washington DC. Kennedy's funeral was attended by 92 foreign leaders and more than a million mourners. His widow, Jackie, lit an eternal flame on his tomb.

25 November 1963, Washington DC, United States
While attending President Kennedy's funeral, Kimberley Sayers was robbed of the Roswell artefact by Majestic agent Phil Albano.

January 1964, Mendoza, Argentina
A UFO was reported to have crashed, killing a number of aliens on board.

Morrison was hell-bent on finding the truth or finding oblivion.

The Doors went on to have many hit records including *Light my Fire* and *People are Strange* in 1967, and a number one hit with *Hello, I Love You* in 1968. The Doors' debut album made number two in the US charts. But despite, or maybe because of, his success, Jim Morrison was dead before he hit thirty.

Morrison's body was found in the bath of his Paris apartment on July 3rd 1971. When an official report was released six days later, he was said to have died of a heart attack induced by respiratory problems. He had apparently visited a doctor that very morning and had coughed up blood later in the day. However, no-one could be certain that this simple explanation was in fact the case since no autopsy was performed on Morrison's body and nobody could find the doctor who had signed his death certificate.

Other explanations for Morrison's sudden demise ranged from a heroin overdose to a long distance death by witchcraft performed by a jilted mistress over in New York. One of Morrison's friends clung to the peculiar belief that he had died while cutting his eyes out to free his spirit. Still more people put forward a conspiracy theory which linked Morrison's death to the deaths of Jimi Hendrix and Janis Joplin. They were all victims of a political conspiracy aimed at eliminating leading members of the hippie movement. Certainly, Morrison had been the subject of a thorough FBI investigation after his arrest on March 1st 1969 for "lewd and lascivious behaviour" during a concert at Dinner Key auditorium. But there are even those who believe that Jim is not dead at all, but that he staged his death to escape his stardom. Whatever the truth may be, a funeral was held at Père Lachaise cemetery later that month. His family were absent, having long since disowned him.

Jim Morrison's tomb was tellingly marked "Kata ton daimona eay toy", which is Greek for "True to his own spirit." (The Last Wave).

MOUNTBATTEN, LOUIS, 1ST EARL MOUNTBATTEN OF BURMA

A British Admiral, last viceroy of India, who served as Chief of the Defence Staff between 1959 and 1965. During this time he saw the merging of the British Army, Navy and Air Force under a unified Ministry of Defence.

Mountbatten's estate, Broadlands, near Romsey in Hampshire, England, was allegedly the site of a UFO landing in February 1955. The landing was witnessed by a member of Mountbatten's staff and the incident later led Mountbatten to observe that it made an irrelevance of the capitalist-communist struggles.

Mountbatten was assassinated in 1979 by the Irish Republican Army.

NASSAU AGREEMENT

This agreement, which assured Anglo-American nuclear collaboration, was signed in Nassau, in the Bahamas, on 18th December 1962. Under this agreement, the US undertook to provide Polaris missiles for British Nuclear submarines.

NATO

The North Atlantic Treaty Organisation was a defence alliance between the Western powers created in 1949 as a response to the growing threat of Soviet control in Eastern Europe. Belgium, Canada, Denmark, France, Great Britain, Iceland, Italy, Luxembourg, the Netherlands, Norway, Portugal and the USA were among the original members of the alliance. Greece, Turkey, Spain and West Germany joined later.

NEW FRONTIER

When President Kennedy was accepted as his party's nomination for Presidential candidate in 1960, he made a speech outlining his hopes and dreams for an America under his presidency. This uplifting speech became known as his "New Frontier" speech, and its message inspired many, like Loengard and Sayers, to put themselves forward to help in the realisation of Kennedy's dreams.

"... we stand today on the edge of a New Frontier – the frontier of the 1960s – a frontier of unknown opportunities and perils – a frontier of unfulfilled hopes and threats ..."

NIXON, RICHARD MILHOUS

Kennedy's opponent during the 1960 Presidential elections, Republican Richard Nixon went on to become President himself in 1968. Nixon was first elected to the House of Representatives in 1947. He served as vice-president under Eisenhower, earning a reputation as a skilful diplomat, and only missed becoming President in 1960 by less than 2 votes per precinct.

When he finally came to power, Nixon set about establishing his "New Economic Policy", aimed at counteracting inflation, which resulted in the devaluation of the dollar both in 1971 and 1973. On the foreign affairs front, Nixon inherited the troubles in Vietnam, but was able to bring the problem to a close (at least for America) in 1973. He made presidential visits to both the Soviet Union and China, bringing about further nuclear arms limitation.

Nixon was re-elected for a second term as President in 1972 but after the "Watergate" scandal of 1973, in which it was discovered that members of Nixon's staff had been ordered to wire-tap the meetings of the Democratic Party's National Committee during the 1972 election campaign, he became the first ever President to resign from office.

NUCLEAR TEST BAN TREATY

One outcome of the Cuban Missile Crisis was that the US and the USSR moved closer to the signing of this treaty, with Britain, in 1963. The signatories agreed not to test nuclear weapons in the atmosphere, or under water, or in outer space.

OSWALD, LEE HARVEY

Became infamous as the man who officially assassinated JFK. According to the Warren Commission, twenty-four-year-old Oswald, a former marine, killed Kennedy with three shots from the sixth floor of the Texas School Book Depository on Elm Street, where he had been working as a clerk. Oswald was already well-known to the security forces. He had become a Soviet citizen in 1959 and was known to be active in the Fair Play for Cuba Committee. (The Awakening, Moving Targets, The Warren Omission).

ORGANIC FREEZE ORBS

These organic pods contain a substance used by the Grays to "freeze" their victims prior to abduction. Kim Sayers was immobilized by one such pod in her bedroom on the night of 21st October 1963. (The Awakening, We Shall Overcome, The Enemy Within).

PALEY, WILLIAM

Head of the CBS network and a member of the Majestic-12 board of directors.

PARKINSON, KENNETH

A BBC technician who was involved in setting

PLANET EARTH TIMELINE
On The Record

17 January 1964, Panama
Panama broke diplomatic relations with the United States.

25 January 1964, United States
Echo 2, a jointly owned American/Soviet satellite, was launched.

PLANET EARTH TIMELINE
Dark Skies

30 January 1964, Florida
Loengard and Sayers travelled to Cape Canaveral to meet the astronaut that Sayers encountered in a recurring dream. (Mercury Rising).

PLANET EARTH TIMELINE
On The Record

30 January 1964, United States
President Johnson and President De Gaulle of France clashed over Vietnam when De Gaulle asserted that the south-east Asian state should remain neutral territory.

PLANET EARTH TIMELINE
Dark Skies

6 February 1964, New York
Loengard and Sayers travelled to New York following a tip-off they received from a Hive broadcast. They arrived at JFK Airport just before The Beatles. (Dark Day's Night).

up the broadcasting equipment for The Beatles' appearance on the Ed Sullivan Show. (Dark Day's Night).

PATIENT ZERO

On February 17, 1962, farmer Elliot Grantham died of apparent head wounds in a car accident seven miles outside Boise, Idaho. During the autopsy on his body however, he was found to have a ganglion, identical to that found inside the Grays at Roswell, attached to the amygdala portion of his brain with tendrils extending throughout his body's central nervous system. This shocking discovery was a turning point for MJ-12, proving unequivocally as it did that the Hive had started to infiltrate the human race. Grantham was subsequently classified for the files as "Patient Zero". (The Awakening).

PENTAGON

Headquarters of the US Defence Services.

POOLE, LANGSTON

Black Baptist minister who was implanted by the Hive and subsequently used the basement of his church as a nursery for growing the organic freeze orbs used by the Grays to immobilise abductees. (We Shall Overcome).

POPEJOY

Majestic agent killed by a chimp which had been implanted with a ganglion for research purposes. Popejoy's death was caught on the Monkey Film. (The Awakening).

POWERS, FRANCIS GARY

US pilot of the U-2 reconnaissance plane which overflew Soviet airspace in May 1962 and was shot down by the Soviets. The incident brought the Paris summit of the time to a halt, while President Eisenhower refused to apologise for the affair. Powers was sentenced to ten years for espionage but was set free early in a hostage swap in exchange for a Soviet spy. (The Awakening).

PRATT, CHARLES

Congressman Pratt from Fresno was Loengard's first congressional employer. After Sayers' abduction, Pratt visited her to introduce her to the "light". When Loengard stumbled in upon them, a fight ensued and Pratt fell to his death from the window of Loengard and Sayers' apartment. (The Awakening, The Warren Omission).

PROJECT BLUE BOOK

Project Blue Book, operated by the US Air Force in response to the "flying saucer" hysteria of the 1950's, went through the motions of investigating civilian and military sightings for almost two decades. Believed by UFO enthusiasts to be conducting a huge cover-up, Blue Book was actually an unwitting pawn of Majestic's secret activities. Although the leadership of Project Blue Book sometimes knew the bigger picture, they were for the most part ignorant of MJ-12's existence and activities.

Project Blue Book was abandoned in 1969, having yielded neither enough proof nor a convincing rationale to justify the continued expenditure of government funds. (The Awakening).

RANKIN, LEE

General Counsel of the Warren Commission. (The Warren Omission).

RAWLINGS

Employee of Howard Hughes at the Desert Inn Hotel and Casino, Las Vegas. (Dreamland).

RICKY

Hive implantee who became part of the Hive's Las Vegas gambling racket. Sayers experienced the Buzz while delivering drinks to this man and his wife in her role as cocktail waitress. (Dreamland).

ROBERTSON PANEL

In 1953, the CIA formed a scientific advisory panel on UFOs at the request of the White House. Members of the panel included Dr. Lloyd Berkner, who is alleged to have been a member of Majestic-12. The panel studied case histories of UFO sightings in the USA and the Soviet Union for just twelve hours before coming to the conclusion that "there was no evidence of a direct threat to national security".

ROCKEFELLER, NELSON ALDRICH

Born in 1908 to the fabulously wealthy Rockefeller family, Nelson Aldrich had already established himself as a philanthropist by founding the Museum of Primitive Art and through his work as trustee of the Museum of Modern Art in New York when he became Republican governor of that city in 1958.

Rockefeller tried and failed to secure the position of Republican Presidential Nominee in 1964 and again in 1968, but he eventually

became vice-president to Gerald Ford in 1974, a position which he held for three years. Nelson Rockefeller died in 1979.

THE ROSWELL INCIDENT

On the 2nd July 1947, hardware dealer Dan Wilmot and his wife were sitting on the porch of their home in Roswell, New Mexico, when they saw a big glowing object flying out at an alarming speed from the south-east. The object was heading north-west towards Corona but before it could reach that city, it was hit by something that made it abruptly change course.

The object may have been hit by a lightning bolt but equally possible is that it was hit by an anti-aircraft missile, given the proximity to Roswell of the White Sands proving grounds and Trinity site and the fact that the object's trajectory would have taken it straight to Los Alamos.

Once hit, the object changed direction towards Socorro, managing to clear the Magdalena/San Mateo Mountains before crashing down to earth near San Agustin.

That the crash was monitored by the military is borne out by the speed with which they responded to the crash. A retrieval team was

10 February 1964, New York City, United States
The Beatles arrived in New York. Crazed fans even mobbed a police officer because he had "touched a Beatle". The Beatles' appearance on the Ed Sullivan show garnered an audience of 73 million. When interviewed, Ringo, the band's drummer, is reputed to have said, "So this is America. They all seem out of their minds."

February 1964, United States
Bob Dylan released "Times they are a changin'".

29 February 1964, United States
The Lockheed corporation announced that it had made a plane capable of flying at 2000 mph.

27 March 1964, Alaska, United States
The Good Friday Quake in Alaska claimed 114 victims.

27 March 1964
Loengard and Sayers arrived in Alaska to investigate the phenomenon of "floating rocks" which had been witnessed near the small town of Chiliwack.

4 April 1964, Panama
Diplomatic relations between Panama and America were resumed.

10 April 1964, Nevada
Loengard and Sayers arrived in Las Vegas in search of work.

(Dreamland)

---

sent out straight away but they failed to gather all the evidence.

William "Mac" Brazel's ranch near Corona had been scattered with wreckage. He reported the debris to the local sheriff who informed Roswell Army Air Base. Brazel was held on the orders of Major Jesse Marcel while the debris collected from his ranch was flown to Wright Patterson Air Force Base. However, this did not happen before several civilians had witnessed the wreckage and even allegedly spoken to the ship's pilot. Witnesses described seeing cables looking like horses' tails, with a light at the end of each strand of hair. This seems to be a description of fibre optic technology, which had yet to be invented on earth.

The following press release was issued by Public Relations Officer Lt. Walter Haut on July 8, 1947:

> *The many rumours regarding the flying disc became a reality yesterday when the intelligence office of 509th Bomb Group of the Eight Air Force, Roswell Army Air Field, was fortunate enough to gain possession of a disc . . . The flying object landed on a ranch near Roswell sometime last week. It was inspected at the Roswell Army Air Field and subsequently loaned by Major Marcel to higher headquarters . . .*

Later, the Army changed their official position to say that the material recovered was not from a "flying saucer" at all but the remains of a wrecked weather balloon. Major Jesse Marcel of the 509th Bomb Squad at Roswell described the material he had seen as thin and foil-like but not able to be dented. There were also fragments of a material similar to balsa wood but which would not burn. Marcel described hieroglyphics on some of the debris, but denied having seen alien bodies, despite subsequent reports that four aliens – known as Grays for the colour of their skin – were on board the wrecked disc. Three of the Grays were dead on arrival. A fourth was allegedly kept alive for a short while at Wright Patterson Air Base but communication was never achieved.

Dark Skies writer Bryce Zabel says of the Roswell cover-up: "*If I were in charge when Roswell happened, I might have done the same thing. It was 1947: we had just fought a nasty bloody war that* threatened all humanity. The Cold War was beginning with nuclear weapons that could eliminate the entire human race. The Iron Curtain had just gone up – and a UFO crashed, outside our only nuclear bomber base. If I was in government at that point, I would have thought twice about saying we should go tell everyone about this. Truman probably did the only thing he felt was responsible, which was to say 'Keep quiet until we get a handle on this'. The only problem was they never actually got a complete handle on it." (The Awakening, Moving Targets, Hostile Convergence).

RUBY, JACK

Owner of the Carousel Club, a strip-joint in Dallas that was used as a Majestic front. Ruby was a Hive implantee, ordered by Jim Steele to kill Lee Harvey Oswald, the man being held for the assassination of JFK. (Moving Targets, We Shall Overcome).

RUSK, DEAN

US Secretary of State from 1961 to 1969. Rusk had particular responsibility for affairs related to the Far East.

SAYERS, ANDREA

Sister of Kimberley Sayers, Andrea became mixed up in the business of Dark Skies when she fell in love and became engaged to a Majestic agent who had become her boyfriend in order to keep tabs on Kimberley. (Hostile Convergence).

SAYERS, JOAN

Mother of Kimberley and Andrea Sayers. (Hostile Convergence).

SAYERS, KIMBERLEY

Ex-White House employee and founder member of Dark Skies. Sayers moved to Washington in 1961 to be with her boyfriend John Loengard. (See additional character/actress profile).

SCHWARZKOPF, CAPTAIN NORMAN

A Majestic operative in Dark Skies, Captain Norman Schwarzkopf rose to fame as "Stormin' Norman" during the Gulf War. (The Warren Omission).

SEATO

The South-East Asia Treaty Organisation was signed in Manila in 1954. The original signatories in this alliance, which extended the US policy of Containment to cover south-east Asia and the South West Pacific, were Australia, Great Britain, France, New Zealand, Pakistan, the Philippines, Thailand and the USA.

SIMONSON, MARK

Loengard's boss during his time as an aide to Congressman Charles Pratt. During the series of Dark Skies, Simonson appears again as a civil rights worker in "We Shall Overcome". Interestingly, the years seem to have dropped off him and Simonson the civil rights worker is about twenty years younger than when we last saw him a year earlier on Capitol Hill. (The Awakening, We Shall Overcome).

SINGULARITY

The moment of empowerment for a group mind. Singularity refers to a threshold point when there will be enough members of the Hive scattered across the Earth to generate a world-wide Hive Mind. When Singularity is achieved, every Hive member will instantaneously know what every other member of the Hive knows and they will be able to move against those humans remaining free from implantation with perfect hostile precision.

Singularity could occur as soon as the late 1990's when the alien consciousness is expected to have enough individual Hives to generate the necessary global/neural interlink. The timing of this event has not been by chance. The Hive intends to complete the neural link-up in time to control the world by the year 2000, capitalising on the human race's subconscious fear of the Millennium.

SMITH, KIM

Sayers uses the psuedonym "Kim Smith" while posing as an anthropology student investigating the phenomenon of the floating rocks in Chiliwack, Alaska. (Ancient Future).

SOCORRO

Small town in New Mexico that became the centre of world attention when Police Officer

11 April 1964, Wisconsin
Farmer Boehm of Monticello, Wisconsin, lost one of his herd of cows after a visitation from the Grays. (Inhuman Nature)

24 April 1964, Socorro, New Mexico
Police patrolman Lonnie Zamora witnessed the landing of a UFO in a quarry just outside Socorro.

Lonnie Zamora sighted a UFO on its outskirts in 1964. (Hostile Convergence).

SOUERS, REAR ADMIRAL SIDNEY

Rear Admiral Sidney Souers was the first Director of Central Intelligence (1946), later becoming Executive Secretary of the National Security Council in 1947, when he also allegedly became one of the original twelve directors of Majestic-12.

SPACE RACE

When the Second World War ended, America found itself in the position of being a true superpower with self-inflicted responsibilities towards the rest of the world, namely keeping vulnerable countries free from communism.

When a US fixed beam radar, based on the Black Sea coast of Turkey, picked up evidence the Soviets were developing ballistic missiles in Stalingrad, the need for America to forge ahead with regard to military technology became even more pressing. Throughout the 1960s, many areas of American life were coloured by the rocket-powered ballistic missile. The discovery that the Soviets were so far ahead left a serious dent in American self-esteem. One of Eisenhower's last actions as President was to ask his government for greater investment in scientific development and the ramifications of his realisation that the gap between the US and the USSR had to be closed were felt in presidential election politics, intelligence gathering, in industry and even in the schools where the scientists of the future were being trained.

A year after the Black Sea radar picked up the bad news from the Soviet Union, Eisenhower's administration was dealt a second blow when October 4th, 1957 saw the launching of Sputnik 1, the first ever artificial satellite. At the time, Eisenhower's advisers called the Sputnik a "silly bauble" and a "basketball in space" but the American satellite operation was immediately stepped up.

The Americans had been designing a much smaller satellite called Vanguard, which could carry a mere twenty pounds to Sputnik's one hundred and eighty four, but before even that was launched, the Soviets pulled off yet another coup, when they rocketed another satellite weighing ten times as much as Sputnik 1 and with a dog on board, into orbit. Poor Laika, the Soviet astrodog, died, but it was clear that the Soviets were going ballistic with their rockets. When Vanguard was finally launched by the US on December 5, 1957, the launch vehicle fell over and exploded two seconds after the fuse was ignited. The Americans got themselves off the ground for the first time on January 31, 1958, when a satellite launched from Cape Canaveral was able to orbit the earth.

The military implications of the Soviets' superior technology were ominous. It was clear that coupled with thermonuclear warheads, the ballistic rocket had become the new king of warfare. After all, if the Soviets could get a satellite weighing over a thousand pounds into orbit from their base at Tyura Tam near the Aral Sea, they could easily send a missile to any point in the United States they pleased. The fear that this might be exactly what the Soviets were planning led to a huge increase in defence spending and the birth of a number of expensive development programs.

An extensive civil space program was put into motion, with funds of 25 billion dollars, which resulted in the famous Apollo flights to the moon.

In the political arena, John F Kennedy capitalised on public fear of Soviet technology and the subsequent "missile gap" which had developed as he fought his presidential election. The first few months of Kennedy's period in office saw yet more Soviet space shocks. On April 12, 1961, Yuri Gagarin sent the whole world into

24 April, 1964, Socorro, New Mexico, United States

Police patrolman Lonnie Zamora was chasing a speeding black Chevrolet when the chase was suddenly interrupted by the bright flash and roar of what Zamora assumed was a dynamite storage shack exploding. Leaving the road to investigate, Zamora's attention was attracted by a shiny object that he took to be an overturned car. However, as he looked more closely, he saw two figures, the size of children, dressed in white coveralls, walking around the object. One of them seemed to spot Zamora and jumped as if he had been surprised.

Thinking that the figures might be in need of help, Zamora went to move his car. But when he next looked up, the figures had vanished. Zamora radioed headquarters to let them know that he was at the scene of a possible accident. As he put down his radio he heard another almighty roar and watched in astonishment as the shiny object shot straight up into the air, shooting out blue and orange flames as it went. Zamora ran for it, thinking that the object was about to blow up, and threw himself into a crash position.

When the roar stopped, Zamora took a hesitant look up and saw that the object was speeding away in a south-westerly direction, just 15 feet above the ground, then, without any further noise, the object lifted itself higher into the sky and disappeared behind the mountains.

Zamora radioed for reinforcements who confirmed that something strange had gone on when they found the marks of what might have been the craft's legs, indented into the rock hard ground. All around the area where Zamora claimed to have seen the peculiar object, the bushes and grass were scorched and still smouldering.

Cynics claimed that the landing marks and the scorching could have been all Zamora's own work, a publicity stunt, aimed at attracting tourists to Socorro, but Zamora was thought by everyone who knew him to be a man of integrity. And, after all, as a policeman, his testimony would usually have been thought honest enough to send someone to jail.

---

shock when he became the first man to orbit the earth. Happening as it did just five days before Kennedy's policy disaster at the Bay of Pigs, Gagarin's flight must have seemed like a real slap in the face, particularly when America's next space venture ended when Alan Shephard made a fifteen minute ballistic flight but never quite made it into orbit.

Twenty days after Shephard's brave but not quite spectacular enough flight, Kennedy announced that the time had come for America to stop messing about. He announced that America would have a man on the moon within ten years and that "No single space project in this period will be more impressive to mankind."

Vice president Lyndon Johnson moved into action straight away, mobilising the administrative and congressional support needed to make Kennedy's dream a reality. It is rumoured that he touted the space program by asking every important White House figure he met "Are you in favour of the US being a second rate nation or are you in favour of this?" Easier goals such as a manned flight around the moon were rejected for fear that the Soviet Union might beat America to such simpler tasks. No, a man on the moon it had to be.

And so the "Space Race" began in earnest. The United States budget for space exploration literally rocketed from $90 million a year under Eisenhower to more than $7.7 billion per annum in the mid-1960s. Thankfully it paid off. The first men on the moon were Americans, Neil Armstrong and Edwin Aldrin, who landed on July 20th 1969.

STEELE, JIM

Jim Steele was a high-ranking agent with Majestic-12 before an unfortunate accident at Majestic headquarters resulted in him being

21 May 1964,
Maryland, United
States
The first nuclear
powered light-
house was opened
in Baltimore, Maryland.

21 June 1964,
Mississippi
Three civil
rights workers
went missing in
mysterious cir-
cumstances after one of them witnessed a Hive ceremony in a Negro
church.

21 June 1964,
Mississippi,
United States
Three civil
rights workers
went missing.
James Chaney, Andrew Goodman and
Michael Schwerner had been stopped
for speeding and taken to Neshoba
County Jail. Upon release, the men
drove to Philadelphia to investigate
the burning of a church. After their
disappearance, fingers were pointed at
the Sheriff's office but no arrests
were made.

3 July 1964, United States
The Civil Rights act was passed to,
in President Johnson's words, "eliminate the last vestiges of injustice
in America."

July 1964, New York City, United
States
Race riots broke out in New York City
after an off-duty police officer
killed a fifteen year old black boy
in Harlem.

implanted by a ganglion extracted from the
amygdala of Patient Zero. Though his condition was discovered, and Bach's men subjected
Steele to ART, the process was unsuccessful
and Steele escaped from Majestic HQ with his
ganglion still intact.

SULLIVAN, ED

A popular light entertainment show host. Ed
Sullivan's show was the vehicle The Beatles
chose for their first live appearance on
American TV. (Dark Day's Night).

SWENSON, SUSAN

A cocktail waitress at the Desert Inn Hotel and
Casino, Las Vegas. Susan witnessed an
exchange of ganglion tendrils between two
Hivers. (Dreamland).

SYNDUCT RESEARCH

A Hive front, Synduct Research conducted
experiments to investigate people's perception
of different types of television advertisements.
In reality, the advertisements contained spliced
in frames of Hive glyphs, which were to be used
to subliminally programme throwbacks to
respond to a later broadcast of the Ed Sullivan
show by committing suicide. (Dark Day's Night).

TAMMY

A hairdresser from Los Angeles who was
implanted and became a Hive stooge in their
Las Vegas gambling racket. (Dreamland).

TAYLOR, LANCE

A black plasterer's apprentice from Meridian,
Mississippi. Taylor became a civil rights worker and was one of three men to go missing during the Freedom Summer. (We Shall
Overcome).

THIRD SHOOTER

Ballistic evidence from the scene of JFK's assassination pointed towards the involvement of
more than one gunman. During The Warren
Omission, Bobby Kennedy sees a film of the
assassination in which the driver of the
President's car turns around to face JFK after
the first two shots have been fired. The film
then shows a spark of light shoot from the
driver's sleeve, suggesting the presence of a
hidden firearm. (The Warren Omission,
Moving Targets).

THROWBACKS

Abductees deemed unsuitable for implantation.
The Hive returns throwbacks to earth after sup-

pressing their memories of the abduction but later tries to kill them (as in Dark Day's Night).

TILLMAN, ETTA MAE

During the "Freedom Summer" of 1964, when the black community of America fought for equal civil rights, Etta Mae sheltered civil rights worker Mark Simonson in her home in Mississippi. (We Shall Overcome).

TLINGIT

A tribe of native Alaskans. Originally nomadic hunters, one group of Tlingit settled in Chiliwack, Alaska, after a spacecraft crash-landed near to their encampment and its Gray pilot begged them to guard the wrecked ship until it "sang its song". The Tlingit appear in Ancient Future.

TOLSON, CLYDE

Clyde Tolson shared a house with J. Edgar Hoover, leading to rumours that they were in fact lovers. (The Warren Omission).

TRUMAN, HARRY S

Harry S. Truman was born on May 8th 1884 to Kansas farming folk. Following a stint at business school, Truman started his working life in the Kansas banks, where he worked variously as a clerk and a bookkeeper. During the period between 1906 and 1917, Truman abandoned the bank for the family farm before joining the National Guard. He saw action in France during the First World War before returning to set up a not-altogether-successful haberdashery firm.

Truman turned to politics in 1924, when he joined the Kansas City Democrats. He worked as a county judge until he was elected to the Senate in 1934. During the Second World War, Truman headed up the Committee to Investigate National Defence, which later became more simply known as the Truman Committee. Then, in 1944, he became vice-president to President Roosevelt, taking on the mantle of President, and the responsibility for dropping the atom bomb on Japan, when Roosevelt died in 1945.

Truman ran for President again in 1948, and was re-elected in a surprise victory over Thomas E. Dewer. Truman's inaugural programme, called the "Fair Deal", guaranteed full employment, a minimum wage and such other goodies as racial equality and public health insurance. Truman did not manage to pass much of his Fair Deal through Congress but among his achievements was the 1949 Housing Act, which provided for low-cost housing. He also ended racial segregation in the armed forces and in federally financed schools.

But Truman is best remembered for his stand against communism, made clear when 1947 saw the publication of the Truman doctrine, though, in 1951, he dismissed General MacArthur for publicly advocating a war against Communist China. Truman also oversaw the US's entry into the NATO pact and committed American troops to the war in Korea under the auspices of the United Nations.

Truman stood down as President in 1953, though he remained politically active until his death in 1972. (The Awakening, Moving Targets).

THE TRUMAN DOCTRINE

Truman's famous doctrine advocating the containment of communism, spoken at a time when Turkey and Greece seemed to be in danger of a communist take-over. In his doctrine, Truman pledged that the USA would "support free peoples who are resisting attempted subjugation by armed minorities or outside pressures", a call to arms which encouraged Congress to vote large sums of military and economic aid to countries seen as vulnerable to the spread of Communism. The Truman Doctrine was seen by the Soviet Union as a declaration of Cold War.

TWINING, GENERAL NATHAN

General Twining was Commanding General of Air Materiel Command, based at Wright-Patterson Air Force Base, when he is alleged to have become one of the original directors of Majestic-12.

UCLA

University of California, Los Angeles. Loengard and Sayers studied at UCLA, as did Jim Morrison, who was a student enrolled at UCLA's School of Cinematography.

12 July 1964, USSR Professor V. Zantser reported seeing a huge disc hovering near his plane on a flight between Moscow and Leningrad.

20 July 1964 Trainee Doctor "Dewey" committed suicide by drinking a bottle of insecticide to combat a hallucinatory swarm of flies that were eating away at his body.

UFO

Short for "Unidentified Flying Object". (See "Flying Saucer").

UNITED NATIONS

Established in 1945, the United Nations replaced the League of Nations as an international organisation working for world peace and security. The Charter of the United Nations was signed by fifty countries in 1945 including the United States and the Soviet Union. More than 100 other nations have since joined.

The United Nations is split into a number of subsidiary organisations to carry out its duties. These include: the General Assembly, where each nation represented has one vote, a Security Council of elected representatives on five year terms who carry out UN policy; a Secretariat to deal with administration; an International Monetary Fund to provide financial assistance to nations in need; and an International Court of Justice.

USSR

The Union of Soviet Socialist Republics. Founded after the Russian Revolution of 1917, the USSR encompassed at its height in the 1960s the whole of northern Asia and much of Eastern Europe, under the legislation of the Supreme Soviet in Moscow. However, since the USSR held its first democratic elections in 1989, it has all but broken down into its constituent republics.

VAN DRUTEN, JACK

One of the twelve directors of Majestic according to Dark Skies.

VANDENBERG, GENERAL HOYT

General Hoyt Vandenberg was Air Force Chief of Staff in 1947, when he is alleged to have become one of the original twelve directors of Majestic-12.

VIETNAM WAR

Once a French colony, Vietnam became independent under Ho Chi Minh in 1945. However, this declaration of independence was followed by French reoccupation and the French Indo-Chinese war which was settled in 1954 at the Geneva Conference. At this conference, Vietnam was partitioned along the 17th parallel, creating a communist Demo-cratic Republic around Hanoi in the north and a non-communist republic around Saigon in the south. However, Ho Chi Minh, who ruled in the north, was committed to reuniting Vietnam as a single communist country and he began a grass roots campaign for his aim, using his Vietcong guerrillas to infiltrate towns in the south.

In 1963, the South Vietnamese leader, Ngo Dinh Diem, was overthrown by his own army. This provided a perfect opportunity for the Vietcong to take advantage of the subsequent political confusion.

The spread of communism in south-east Asia was of grave concern to the US, who had cast themselves in the role of protectors of the vulnerable countries from Bolshevik ways. The United States became involved in the Vietnam War in 1964, after the "Gulf of Tonkin" incident, in which US ships were allegedly attacked by the North Vietnamese. President Johnson used this incident to gain congressional support for further military action and by 1967, 400,000 US soldiers were fighting the Vietnam War.

However, the US army were no match for the guerrilla tactics of the Vietcong, who knew the Vietnamese jungles and could blend in with South Vietnamese to avoid detection. The war limped on, with heavy US casualties, until the Paris Peace Accord of January 1973 saw US troops finally withdraw from this unwinnable conflict. No settlement was made between the North and South Vietnamese and on April 30, 1975, Saigon finally fell to the North Vietnamese.

WARING, MARK

A trainee veterinary surgeon at the University of Wisconsin, Madison. Waring performed a necropsy on a mutilated cow from Kester Boehm's Gray-visited farm. Waring later operated on a live cow from the same farm to remove a human foetus which was being incubated inside its third, or ruminant, stomach.

WARREN COMMISSION

A commission formed to investigate the circumstances surrounding the assassination of President Kennedy. After much deliberation, the Warren Commission came to the conclusion that Lee Harvey Oswald had acted alone and that there was no conspiracy involved.

WARREN, CHIEF JUSTICE EARL

Leader of the Warren Commission. (The Warren Omission).

WARSAW PACT

The Warsaw Pact, more formally known as the Warsaw Treaty of Friendship, Co-operation and Mutual Alliance, was signed in 1955. It constituted a military alliance between the Soviet-bloc countries of Albania, Bulgaria, Czechoslovakia, the German Democratic Republic, Hungary, Poland, Romania and the Soviet Union, believed to be a direct response to the inclusion of West Germany in NATO. Members of the pact were required to maintain Soviet Army units within their borders, under a unified military control, which could be called upon for the mutual assistance of any member state.

WEATHERLY, CHRISTOPHER JR.

A student who participated in an experiment in New York during which he was brain-washed to respond to the stimulus of a Beatles song by committing suicide. It appeared that Christopher Weatherly Jr. has been abducted by the Grays but was returned to earth unimplanted as a "throwback". (Dark Day's Night).

WEATHERLY, CHRISTOPHER SR.

Father of Christopher Weatherly Jr., Christopher Sr. was abducted at the same time as his son, but unlike his son, he was implanted with a ganglion. Christopher Sr. helped Hive members infiltrate the set of the Ed Sullivan show where he was working as a janitor. (Dark Day's Night).

WELLER, ROB

A Majestic agent sent to infiltrate Sayers' family by becoming the boyfriend of her sister, Andrea. Weller subsequently fell in love with Andrea, proposed marriage and admitted his Majestic connections to her.

WHITMAN

Proprietor of Whitman Bros. Funeral Home, Los Angeles, where the body of Dewey, the young doctor who died as a result of ingesting insecticide, was held. (The Last Wave).

YOUNT, TY

An astronaut in NASA's covert operation, Midnight Wing, Yount flew with co-pilot Gary Augatreux on the supposedly unmanned Gemini mission which encountered the Hive mother ship. Yount, with Augatreux, was taken into the Hive ship but was not implanted with a ganglion. Instead Yount became a throwback, plagued by recurring dreams about his experience in which he saw Kim Sayers, who was abducted from her Washington home on the same night. (Mercury Rising).

ZAMORA, LONNIE

Zamora was working as a police officer in Socorro, New Mexico when a series of bright flashes and loud bangs led him to a quarry where he encountered a spacecraft that appeared to have been piloted by two humanoid beings. His sighting of an "egg-shaped" craft, piloted by something other than Grays, led to speculation that the USAF had recreated a spacecraft using plans of the ship found at Roswell.

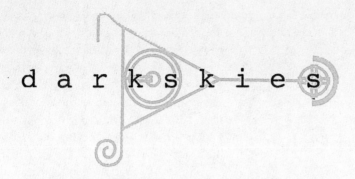

d a r k s k i e s

CHARACTER PROFILES
John Loengard

The name "Loengard" is a play on words. From "Loengard" comes "Lone Guard", the single sentry at the gate to the truth. It is the name that Bryce Zabel gave to the anonymous correspondent who first suggested to him that history might not have been exactly as we remember it.

The John Loengard of *Dark Skies* is an idealistic twenty-four year old UCLA graduate when he heads to Washington DC in 1961 to start on the career path which he hopes might one day lead him to the tenancy of the White House itself. Loengard finds himself a job in the office of Senator Pratt, senator for Fresno, John's home town, and things seems to be going well when John's boss, Mark Simonson, gives him the opportunity to stretch himself by investigating a number of minor government organisations in order to be able to make a recommendation as to which could be scrapped in an attempt to save money.

But Loengard's very conscientiousness finally gets the better of him. While making a report on Project Blue Book, the government's official agency for the investigation of UFOs, Loengard stumbles across the testimonies of Barney and Betty Hill, who claim that they had been abducted from their car by aliens. Loengard decides that, ridiculous as their story sounds, he can't make a proper judgement about it until he hears the story from the couple's own mouths. He visits them at their home, hears their story, and his life is changed forever. What possible reason could these two people have to make such a story up, he wonders. Particularly since they are a mixed race couple already open to more abuse than they need. But before Loengard can pass his decision on to Senator Pratt, he is silenced, dramatically, by a group of men who arrive from nowhere in an unmarked helicopter and force him off the road.

This is Loengard's first encounter with Majestic-12. A fright and a fight, that leaves him fearing for his life. But not so scared that he doesn't delve even deeper into the mysterious world of ufology on his return to Washington. Eventually, when it becomes clear that Loengard is a man who has to have the truth at any price, Captain Frank Bach of Majestic has no choice but to make Loengard one of his own.

From then on Loengard is sentenced to a double life. Even when he decides to quit Majestic because he disagrees with their policy of keeping the truth even from the President for the sake of National Security, Loengard cannot leave behind the reality that the Hive is already infiltrating the human race. With his girlfriend Kim Sayers, who was rudely informed of the Hive's presence by a night on a Gray ship that left her with a ganglion in the head, Loengard goes on the run.

Loengard is too honest for the clandestine ways of Majestic-12. He finds it impossible to believe that it is in the best interests of everyone for even President Kennedy to be kept firmly in the dark. In Loengard's opinion, how can the human race possibly hope to defeat the Hive if they aren't allowed to know their enemy? But as we watch him chase all over the United States in the Hive's wake, it is also clear that Loengard appreciates that the truth about the Hive is not something that can be announced to the

On The Record

31 July 1964, United States
4,000 photographs of the lunar landscape were beamed back from Ranger 7 before it crash-landed on the moon.

August 1964, Vietnam
America claimed that two of her destroyers had been the victims of attacks by the North Vietnamese in the Gulf of Tonkin Incident. Truman demanded broad emergency powers and the South East Asia resolution became law. This vaguely worded document gave Johnson congressional authority to "take all necessary measures to repel any armed attack against the forces of the US and to prevent further aggression." However, the resolution was not popular throughout the Senate and there were rumours that the attacks had never happened and that Johnson was merely using the resolution as a pretext to expand his powers.

4 August 1964, Mississippi, United States
The partially decomposed bodies of three men were discovered in an earthen dam near Philadelphia, Mississippi. The men were identified as civil rights workers James Chaney from Meridian, and Andrew Goodman and Michael Schwerner from New York City, who had been missing since 21 June 1964.

world like the latest football score. He appreciates that the truth will be terrifying for most people. It needs to be approached from the top down. The government must have a strategy in place so that a solution can be offered along with the problem. The question is, how to convince the government that there is a problem when Majestic-12 has covered its tracks so carefully that many people at the top level of government don't even know that Majestic exists, let alone the Hive.

When casting the part of John Loengard, Zabel and Friedman looked for someone who could embody the innocence and idealism of the early 1960s, someone with faith in the ultimate goodness of the human race. He needed to be an "Everyman." As much as it is a story about the fight to overcome the Hive, *Dark Skies* is about the loss of innocence, which is personified by John Loengard as he struggles to come to terms with the new horrors he uncovers every day.

The role of Loengard eventually went to Eric Close, a veteran of the small screen who is best remembered for his role in the series "Sisters". He has also had roles in "McKenna" and "Taking Liberty", and made guest appearances on "Major Dad" and "McGyver". Close has starred in a number of made for television movies including "Stranger Beside Me", "Without Consent", "Hercules" and "Keeping Secrets". His feature film credits include "American Me", which was directed by Edward James Olmos, and "Safe House".

When he isn't fighting the Hive, Close makes time for his other interests. He is a keen tennis player and also enjoys skiing, rock-climbing and fly-fishing.

Of the series, Close says that: "*Dark Skies* is an allegory for the evil (or ganglion) within us all."

19 August 1964
Loengard and Sayers returned to Loengard's family home in Fresno to cash some bonds that would enable them to continue their mission. However, they soon discovered that Ray, Loengard's brother, had been implanted by the Hive. (The Enemy Within)

20 September 1964
Loengard and Sayers were summoned to Washington by the Attorney-General Robert Kennedy to give evidence to the Warren Commission. (The Warren Omission)

DARK SKIES: THE OFFICIAL GUIDE

Kimberley Sayers

The character of Kimberley Sayers is a complex and multi-layered one. When the series begins in 1961, it quickly becomes clear that Sayers is no ordinary all-American Girl. She has followed her lover to Washington DC and moves in with him while she searches for a job. Despite the curtains which are doubtless ready to twitch across her new neighbourhood, Sayers shuns the idea of getting married, saying that she wants to find out who Kim Sayers is before she becomes Mrs. Loengard.

But Sayers' attempt at making the mythological freedom of the 1960s a reality is rudely cut short when she is abducted from her bedroom by the Grays and subsequently implanted with a ganglion. Though Loengard manages to force the ganglion to leave Sayers' body using ART, things can never be the same again. The small stand that Sayers thought she was making by maintaining her independence as a single woman suddenly seems unimportant when she faces up to her new role in the defence of the human race. In fact, by the time Loengard and Sayers face the horror of cattle being used to incubate human babies in Monticello, Sayers would give anything for the chance to be Mrs. Loengard, with a picket fence and healthy children. Faced with so much uncertainty, she longs for the normality she once poo-poohed.

The part of Kimberley Sayers is played by Megan Ward. Though she is only in her twenties, Los Angeles-born Ward has already had a long career in the public eye. She began modelling at the age of fifteen and quickly became a hit in Japan, where she co-hosted her own television series. A feature

27 September 1964, Washington DC, United States
The Warren Commission, set up by President Johnson to investigate the assassination of President Kennedy, released its conclusions. Led by Chief Justice Earl Warren, the Commission ruled that the assassination suspect, Lee Harvey Oswald, had fired three shots from the sixth floor of the Texas School Book Depository, Elm Street, Dallas. They further concluded that Oswald had acted alone. The report then went on to make the assassination of a president or vice-president a federal crime and reprimanded the FBI for not having alerted the Secret Service to Oswald's presence in Dallas despite the fact that he was known to be a member of the "Fair Play for Cuba" Committee.

3 November 1964, United States
Lyndon Johnson retained the presidency of the United States with a landslide victory.

10 December 1964
Martin Luther King became the youngest ever recipient of the Nobel Peace Prize.

film career followed, with parts in "Joe's Apartment", "Cruz", "Freaked" and "Amityville V". She also starred in "The Brady Bunch Movie", "Encino Man" and "Goodbye Paradise" and her television credits include guest starring roles on such hit series as "The Single Guy", "Party of Five" and the critically acclaimed "Sweet Justice".

November 1965, United States Eight states — Connecticut, Massachusetts, Maine, New Hampshire, New Jersey, New York, Pennsylvania and Vermont — lost power in this historical power failure which became known as the Great Northeast Blackout. A faulty automatic relay device at a plant near Niagara Falls was blamed but there is evidence that UFOs can cause power failures, although this may only be a side effect rather than an intentional act. Specifically, the Great Northeast Blackout is thought to have been instigated by the Hive to prevent the airing of the "Monkey Film" on national television. Later that year, grid systems failed in New Mexico and Texas following UFO sightings in those areas.

1975, United States The Robertson Panel's report on UFOs was finally declassified. While debunking the UFO "myth", it turns out that the report had recommended that Eisenhower's government take steps to quash UFO reports with an anti-UFO education campaign, which might perhaps be delivered in the form of cartoons by the Walt Disney Studios. It also recommended that UFO enthusiast groups be placed under surveillance to avoid the "possible use of such groups for subversive purposes".

Despite this huge diversity of roles, Ward has a special place in her heart for Kimberley Sayers. The role of an independent woman of the 1960's fascinates Ward and she feels that the storylines of the first *Dark Skies* series challenge her on many levels. Sayers has to change quickly from a carefree career girl, challenging social boundaries, to a heroine carrying a secret which is a great weight on her heart. Ward says of Sayers, "What happens to her is really tragic, but I think there is an adventurous side to Kimberley . . . She has to be a bit of a daredevil at heart, because if she isn't, the world's going to end. It's always a balance making these character qualities real and believable, then relating them to the situations and how they can change the future." So it's a difficult part to play, perhaps more so than the role of Loengard, who at least isn't struggling against social expectations of his sex as well as the Hive, but Ward concludes: "The writers have slowly made Kimberley stronger and stronger, and I like that. As long as she continues to progress, to be challenged . . . I'll be happy."

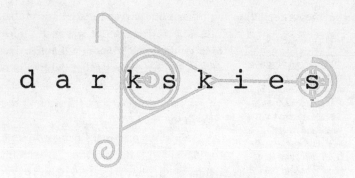

d a r k s k i e s

THE WRITERS

Bryce Zabel and his writing partner Brent Friedman believe in UFOs. They believe that a spacecraft of unknown origin crashed in the New Mexico desert outside Roswell Army Air Base on July 2 1947 and that ever since that world-changing event, someone has been covering up.

Zabel began his wide and varied career in local news and was the first Los Angeles-based on-camera correspondent for CNN, covering events from presidential campaigns to space shuttle launches. He later became an investigative reporter for the PBS/ KCET program "News Beat" and won an award for exposing medical malpractice. But Zabel's nose for the truth led him to stumble upon something truly shocking in 1989, while he was writing a telefilm based on the legendary events at Roswell, called *Official Denial*.

Inexplicable

1979, United States
Major Jesse Marcel, who had been the intelligence officer of the 509th Bomb Group at Roswell in 1947, spoke to a journalist about his experience as Roswell. He confirmed that the material found in the New Mexico desert was definitely not the remains of a weather-balloon.

1984, Los Angeles, California
Hollywood producer Jaime Shandera received an anonymous package containing documents pertaining to be proof of the existence of Majestic-12.

During the course of his research into Roswell, Zabel spoke with many ex-servicemen who had actually worked on the base during 1947. Their stories of that fateful night tallied all too closely with the literature that Zabel had hitherto thought of as fiction. And when the film was actually released, the tale took an even stranger turn. Zabel received a letter from an unnamed correspondent who informed him that "You have a pretty good movie but you kind of go off the rails at the end." The correspondent implied that he knew more than the official line about Roswell and Zabel agreed to meet with him. The correspondent was in his mid- to late-fifties, and when he still refused to give Zabel his name, Zabel dubbed him "John Loengard", a pun on "lone guard", the single sentry, the man at the gate to the truth.

1989, Las Vegas, United States

A man named Bob Lazar, claiming to be a physicist who had worked at Area 51, went live on a Las Vegas TV station to announce that he had been involved in the "re-engineering" of extraterrestrial spacecraft. The spacecraft were kept in underground hangars at Papoose Lake, just to the south of Area 51, but had been used in test runs over the Area 51 region itself.

Lazar's claims were neither con- firmed nor denied by the US Air Force, who maintain that Area 51 does not exist. However, Lazar's personal history could be checked out, and his claim that he was educated at MIT and Cal-Tech was not backed up by records of attendance at either institution. Lazar's supporters have accused the authorities of removing Lazar's educa- tional records in an attempt to dis- credit him.

After their meeting, Loengard wrote to Zabel and his partner Friedman, telling them that they should write the series *Dark Skies*, based on the things that Loengard had told them. Loengard advised Zabel and Friedman that they had been specially selected to tell the truth through fiction. He ended his letter by saying "This is the only way. Don't be afraid. The future of humanity demands your courage."

Zabel and Friedman set to work, laying out the events of UFO mythology alongside important events from world history in a timeline that threw up some startling connections. The work led Friedman to describe history as a "rolled-up tapestry". By creating their alternative timeline, Zabel and Friedman were "stretching it out . . . and finding all of those hidden stories. The more you look back, the more you find that there is a secret history."

If the idea that the Kennedy assassination, Vietnam, the fight for civil rights and the space race can all be connected by the malevolent influence of an alien nation, the Hive, still seems outlandish, then Zabel has this sobering conclusion. "Americans have been lied to a number of times about big issues – the Kennedy assassination, Vietnam, Watergate, Iran-Contra, nuclear tests and so on . . . Why not UFOs? If you believe that a spacecraft crashed at Roswell in 1947 – and the evidence is relatively strong that something happened – then almost anything is possible . . . And that's the scariest thought of all."

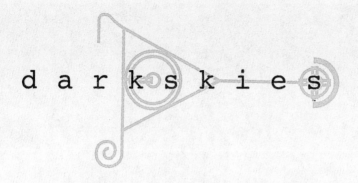

PRODUCER PROFILE
James D. Parriott

The Executive Producer of *Dark Skies*, James D. Parriott began his career in television as a staff writer at Universal Television in the early 1970s, where he contributed to such hugely popular series as the "Six Million Dollar Man", "The Bionic Woman" and "The Incredible Hulk", for which he was also the supervising producer. Since then he has written and directed "American Girls" and created the series "Matt Waters". His most recent television series was "The Invaders".

Parriott's movie credits include "The Legend of the Golden Gun", "Island Sons" for Universal, and "Staying Afloat" for Tri-Star.

1991, United States
Following the airing of his television programme about the Roswell Incident, writer Bryce Zabel received an anonymous letter from someone claiming to know the truth about that night. When Zabel met the man, he was inspired to create Dark Skies with his writing partner Brent V. Friedman, when the anonymous man, dubbed Loengard, told them that they had a duty to bring the "truth" to the attention of the world.

SPECIAL EFFECTS

T he special effects for *Dark Skies* were provided by two different companies. The first, the Todd Masters Company, whose credits include "Predator", "Mortal Kombat" and "Star Trek: First Contact", created both the Grays and the ganglions. Of these creatures, Masters said, "We're a bit limited with what we can have the alien robots do because they are somewhat humanoid, but ganglions are really not of this earth – pardon the pun – so we can come up with bizarre ideas of how they attack people and crawl out through human bodies and explode out of faces. That's the fun stuff."

The spaceship effects are the work of Area 51, a company led by Visual Effects Supervisor Tim McHugh. Unlike the Todd Masters Company, Area 51 use computers to generate most of their effects and Tim McHugh says of *Dark Skies*, "The process of creating these effects is painstaking. I sometimes feel that computer artists are like the monks of old who used to copy out religious texts one letter at a time – the process isn't that interesting to watch, but the results are impressive." As anyone who watches the series would have to agree.

1993, Nevada, United States
The US Air Force annexed a piece of land known as Freedom Ridge, which overlooked Groom Lake, the alleged location of Area 51. The Freedom Ridge had become a popular hang-out for UFO enthusiasts after Bob Lazar's 1989 television announcement that UFOs were being taken for test-runs at Groom Lake.

1993, United States
US Congressman Steven Schiff of New Mexico asked for a full report into the Roswell Incident. The matter was taken up by the General Accounting Office, the investigative branch of Congress.

d a r k s k i e s

FILMING DARK SKIES

Though the episodes in the first series of *Dark Skies* are set in American states as far apart and wildly different in climate and scenery as Alaska and Florida, most of the series was filmed in Greater Los Angeles. This locational restriction led to a number of headaches for the series' production designers Greg Melton and Curtis A. Schnell, who had to spend weeks driving around to find parts of Los Angeles that could masquerade as New York or Idaho. Once that was done, they then had the further worry of making the California locations look like these other states in the 1960s, without going over the budget or time-span of the tight TV schedule.

One of the biggest problems for the production designers was making real interiors, such as that used for the Sayers' family home, look period. Here they struggled with light fittings and other appliances that were too modern to remain in shot. The clothes and the cars were the easy part, with experts in each area knowing exactly who would be wearing or driving what, almost down to the right month. Getting the cars right, said Melton, is about 50% of the work involved in making a street shot look right.

162

Scenes with large amounts of effects work were generally shot in specially built sets in studios. For example, a special set was built for the scenes in the church basement in "We Shall Overcome", since real basements are notoriously difficult to shoot in because of the difficulty of getting lights and equipment into such confined spaces.

When all the location problems had been sorted out, each episode of the first series was shot over approximately eight days, with the first few episodes going out before the series was even finished. No wonder an exhausted Megan Ward said of the series, "It is a very ambitious show."

September 1994, United States
The United States Air Force issued a report entitled "Report of Air Force Research Regarding the 'Roswell Incident'", which denied that the Air Force had covered up the retrieval of an alien spacecraft during 1947.

1997, United States and Europe
"Dark Skies" hits the television screens, presenting the "truth" as fiction, in a dissection of world history prepared to take us from Roswell to the Millennium with the scales lifted from our eyes.

IN CONCLUSION
History Hot-Spots

Dark Skies

On The Record

Inexplicable

At first sight, a time-line laying out events from the annals of ufology alongside moments in history that we are sure we know to have happened can seem a little bewildering. The connections aren't always immediately obvious. For instance, what does the foundation of the CIA have to do with the recovery of the wreckage of a weather balloon outside Roswell, New Mexico? You don't have to scratch very deep to find that one event throws a very different complexion on the other.

The year 1947 in particular is full of examples where history collides head-on with UFO mythology. With the advantage of hindsight and startling new evidence that has come to light in the last decade through the Freedom of Information Act, the result of pairing the two views of the past is perhaps a clearer truth than we might have imagined possible.

Four months before Roswell, in March 1947, Truman asked Congress for $400 million to support the stand against communism in Turkey and Greece. Less than two weeks later he asked for a further $25 million, this time to carry out security checks on all members of the FBI for, amongst other things, tendencies towards communism. But was Truman really arming the United States against communism, or was he using communism to hide the terrifying face of his real mission, to defend the world from a threat far worse than Stalin?

Did Majestic really exist?

After the so-called "Roswell Incident", which was officially written off as the discovery of wreckage from a weather balloon, Truman took two more decisive steps to ensure the security of his nation. Less than a month after Roswell, Truman brought all the armed forces together under the control of James V. Forrestal, then in September of the same year he sanctioned the creation of the new Central Intelligence Agency under the direction of Rear Admiral Roscoe Hillenkoetter.

These two men, Forrestal and Hillenkoetter, provide the link to one of the most contentious issues in US military intelligence history – Majestic-12. Its existence has long been denied by the US Government, but in 1984 Hollywood producer Jaime Shandera received a startling piece of mail suggesting that Majestic-12 was alive and kicking in the late 1940s and early 1950s when Truman went defense crazy, allocating 75% of his final budget to arms and signing treaties of alliance with any world leaders who would sit still for long enough. Shandera's astonishing discovery claimed that, as well as being two of the most important men in the US Military, Forrestal and Hillenkoetter were members of Majestic-12's board of twelve directors.

The anonymous parcel that Shandera received in 1984 contained an unexposed roll of film. When the film was developed, Shandera found himself in possession of photographs of two documents. The first was a memo, written on 24 September 1947, to James V. Forrestal from President Truman himself. The second was a 1952 briefing document, from Rear Admiral Roscoe Hillenkoetter to the President-elect, Dwight Eisenhower.

The memo from President Truman authorised the implementation of "Operation Majestic Twelve". The briefing paper, which was classified as "Top Secret/Majic/Eyes Only", is a summary of UFO intelligence from 1947 to 1952, and includes details about Roswell. It also details the names of all twelve members of the original Majestic board. Roscoe and Hillenkoetter were backed up by men from the very highest levels of defense and research: Dr. Lloyd Berkner, Executive Secretary of the Joint Research and Development Board; Dr.

Detlev Bronk, chairman of the National Research Council; Dr. Vannevar Bush, leader of the Manhattan Project which developed the first atomic bomb; Gordon Gray, Assistant Secretary of the Army; Dr. Jerome Hunsaker, Chairman of the National Advisory Committee for Aeronautics; Dr. Donald Menzel, Director of the Harvard College Observatory; General Robert Montague, commander of the Sandia Base, New Mexico; Rear Admiral Sidney Souers, Executive Secretary of the National Security Council; General Nathan Twining, Commanding General at Wright Patterson Air Force Base; and General Hoyt Vandenberg, Director of Central Intelligence.

The authenticity of Shandera's document has, of course, been questioned, but the first reaction of Richard M. Bissell Jr, ex-CIA Deputy Director of Plans and a member of the White House Staff during the Truman administration, was that the document was real. Other anecdotal evidence supports this claim. UFO researcher William Steinman was even warned off the subject of Majestic-12 by Dr. Eric Walker, a British scientist who had served as Executive Secretary of the Research and Development Board, after Dr. Walker had admitted that he had been present at meetings at Wright-Patterson Air Force Base where the assembled discussed not only the recovery of UFOs, but what should be done with recovered alien bodies.

What really happened at Roswell?

So if Majestic-12 really existed and has been kept secret for so long, it stands to reason that the official line on Roswell may not reflect what really happened on the night of July 2nd 1947.

The briefing paper which came to be in the possession of a Hollywood producer so mysteriously may offer some clues. Allegedly, the paper describes that an aerial reconnaissance mission on the night of 2nd July recorded the ejection of "four small human-like figures" from the Roswell craft. The bodies were not found for a further week, during which time they became badly decomposed and damaged by predators. However, the bodies were subjected to analysis in "A covert effort", headed by General Twining and Dr. Bush on the orders of President Truman. Dr. Bronk's conclusion on the origin of the creatures was that "the biological and evolutionary processes responsible for their development (were) quite different from those observed and postulated in homo-sapiens." It was Dr. Bronk who dubbed the creatures "EBEs", Extraterrestrial Biological Entities.

The likes of Jesse Marcel, who was an intelligence officer in the 509th Bomb Group, the atomic-bomb unit that had its home at Roswell Army Air Field, were kept unaware that any bodies had been found, but it was a difficult secret to keep when civilians were involved. Glenn Dennis, who worked as a mortician at a funeral home near the base, recalls being asked about the availability of hermetically sealed coffins for "future use". Dennis learned more from his girlfriend, a nurse at the base, who claimed that she had been present for the autopsy of the EBEs. The nurse was later transferred to England and allegedly killed in a plane crash of which no record has ever been found.

Whatever the real story is, it seems odd that the crash of a weather balloon should have been surrounded by so much secrecy and that the wreckage of the said balloon should have been transported from place to place under armed guard.

The case was reopened in the 1990s when US Congressman Steven Schiff of New Mexico asked for a full report. The matter was taken up by the General Accounting Office, the investigative branch of Congress, but before they were able to release their findings, the Air Force issued a preemptive report which stated that "The post-War US military (or today's for that matter) did not have the capability to rapidly identify, recover, co-ordinate, cover-up and quickly minimise public scrutiny of such an event. The claim that they did so without leaving even a little bit of a suspicious paper trail for 47 years is incredible."

The Beginning of the End?

Perhaps the idea that the US military could have covered up an alien landing is incredible, but it could be that even the Air Force report of the 1990's was subject to Majestic's veto and thus bound to deny the existence of UFOs .

Whatever the case, something definitely seems to have happened in 1947. Roswell was not the only alleged sighting of an alien craft that year. In June, Kenneth Arnold sighted twenty-five brass coloured objects over the Grande Valley in Oregon. In July, the crew of a DC-3 over Idaho encountered five UFOs. In September, the flight crew of a civilian flight to Honolulu encountered a glowing object over the Pacific Ocean. And it wasn't just happening in America. In France, there was a marked upsurge in sightings of the Virgin Mary (believed by many to be an alien herself, as evidenced by the Immaculate Conception and the return from the dead of her son Jesus Christ).

The next year, 1948, was also a bumper year for sightings over or near US Air Force bases. If there was nothing to worry about, what on earth possessed Brigadier General C.P. Cabell to request that every military base in America be equipped with an interceptor-type aircraft for the express purpose of chasing UFOs? And why, in the February of 1949, was the National Laboratory at Los Alamos the venue for a conference to discuss UFO phenomena?

The early 1950s were no less busy on the UFO front, producing legislation to cover the manner in which UFOs should be reported, and, allegedly, the foundation of the "Interplanetary Phenomenon Unit". General MacArthur is even said to have gone so far as to announce that "The nations of the world will have to unite for the next war will be an interplanetary war". Not long after MacArthur's statement, the Soviet Union united with eight other Soviet countries in the Warsaw Pact. A response to the news that West Germany had been allowed to join NATO, or to the rise in the number of sightings in Soviet airspace since 1947?

In the late 1950's and the early 1960's, the so-called "Cold War" escalated dramatically. The Americans discovered that the Soviets were developing ballistic missiles, and then the Soviets managed to launch the first ever artificial satellite months before the US was able to respond in kind. Politicians in the United States feared that a "missile gap" would leave them at the mercy of the Soviets. And the UFO sightings continued, one of the most notable being over the headquarters of a tactical missile organisation at Sverdlorsk in the USSR in 1959, when a UFO circled the site for twenty-four hours. Two years later, the Soviet missile base was again the focus of much inexplicable activity, including sightings of a disc-shaped object and the disappearance of the entire crew and all the passengers on one of the base's planes, though the plane was later found intact.

A widely-held theory that the increase in UFO sightings since 1947 could be due to the increase in military technology is supported by the Sverdlorsk mysteries. The theory holds that aliens have been attracted to the earth by our experiments with atomic energy in particular. Some even believe that the visitations to atomic missile bases were intended as warnings that the deployment of such missiles could cause widespread damage and misery, and not just on Planet Earth.

Another theory, espoused by *Dark Skies*, is that the aliens are looking for our Achilles Heel. They will have no need to sweep in and fight us for our resources if they can carefully manipulate the weaknesses we already have and use them to set us at each other's throats. Certainly it seems that as we approach the Millennium, the human race finds itself in a period of unprecedented uncertainty and insecurity. Many believe that this period started in the 1960's, when the world "lost its innocence". It seemed that every status quo was being challenged then: racial equality, sexual equality, political ideologies. People began to question the right of the government to keep them in the dark about things "for their own good". But perhaps it was really the case that even the President of the United States didn't have access to the full story.

The briefing document from Rear-Admiral Roscoe Hillenkoetter that shed so much light on the Majestic-12 issue took almost forty years to emerge from its top-secret vault. Perhaps by the end of this century, something will come to light that answers the remaining questions that abound in twentieth century history. Until that happens – Watch the Skies.

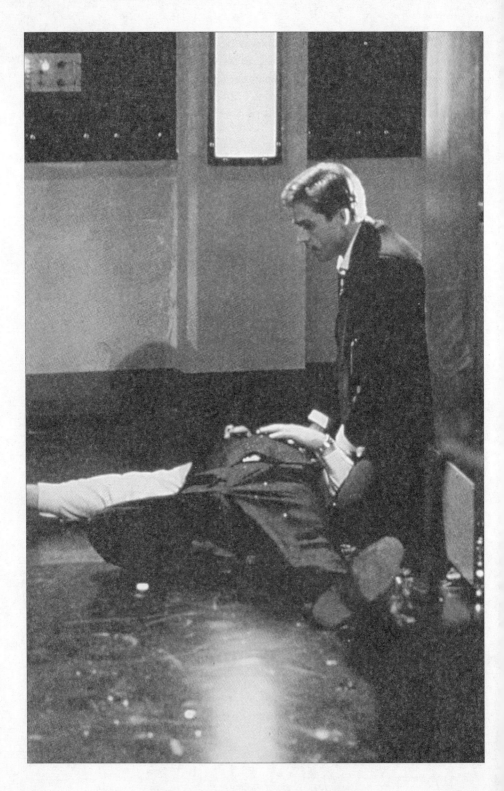

PRODUCTION CREDITS
The Awakening

(2 hour pilot)

Costumes : Jennifer Parsons	*Production Accountant* : Steve Beeson
Music : Mark Snow	*Camera Operator* : Pernell Tyus
Film Editor : Andrew Cohen ACE	*1st Assistant Camera* : Alex Touyart
Production Designer : Curtis A Schnell	*Gaffer* : Dave Maddux
Director of Photography : Bill Butler ASC	*Key Grip* : Richard Jones
Produced by : Bruce Kerner	*Loader* : Luke Stern
Co-executive producer : Brent V Friedman	*Sound Mixer* : Marty Bolger
Executive producer : Joseph Stern	*Post Production*
Executive producer : Bryce Zabel	*Co-ordinator* : Bonnie Stern
Written by : Bryce Zabel and	*Assistant Editor* : Ron Shaw
Brent V Friedman	*Transportation*
Director : Tobe Hooper	*Co-ordinator* : Jeri Kelly
Co-producer : Bernie Laramie	*Construction Co-ordinator* : Alun Vick
Casting : Judith Holstra CSA	*Assistant to Producers* : Eric Kaufman
Special Effects : Todd Masters	Adam Sigel
Unit Production Manager : Larry Kostroff	"Flip" Filippelli
1st Assistant Director : Richard Scher	*Assistant to Mr. Hooper* : Michael Hoffs
2nd Assistant Director : Jeffrey Snednick	*2nd Assistant Director* : Tamu Blackwell
Stunt Co-ordinator : John Moio	*Production Assistants* : Michelle Dupont
Visual Effects Supervisor : Joe Rayner	Blue Nelson
Special Effects : Larry Fioritto	Arthur Scott
Make-up : Joyce Westmore	Jeffrey Jones
Alan Friedman	*Colorist* : Randy Starnes
Hair : Sher Flowers	*Sound Supervisor* : Eric Hoien
Make-up/Wardrobe : Victoria de Kay	*Sound Effects Design* : Dave A Davis
Set Decorator : Christa Schneider	*Re-recording Mixers* : Sherry Klein
Script Supervisor : Helen Pinkston	Bob Edmondson
Production Co-ordinator : Ellen Wolff	Joel Fein
Debra Olchick	*Music Editor* : Marty Wereski
Location Manager : Tim Hillman	*Casting Associate* : Ken Miller
Property Master : Brad Breitbarth	*Walla Group* : Joshua Stein

Production Manager DC : Carol Flaisher
Production
Co-ordinator DC : Theresa Rubino
2nd Assistant Director : Alison Rosa

Alien Effects by the Todd Masters Company
Animatronic
Project Heads : Scott Tebeau
Luke Khanlian
Scott Coulter
Greg Johnson
David Matherly
Alien Effects
Co-ordinator : Kristine Morgan
Todd Masters Co. Crew : Jaremy Aiello
Mark Boley
Tim Huizing
Mark Dillon
Bill Fesh
Thomas Kileen
Dana Klaren
Chris Koranet
Vince Niebla
Walter Phelan
John Shea
Matthew Singer

Todd Masters Co. Crew : Shanna Tebeau
A J Venuto

Special Visual Effects by Sony Pictures
Imageworks
CG Producer : Frank Foster
CG Supervisor : Matt Hausle
Visual Effects
Co-ordinator : Fiona Bul
Technical Assistants : Ian Wosiski
Animators : John Bevelheimer
Michael Sanchez
Bill Diaz
Martin Foster
Rachel Nicoll
David Schaub
David Worman
Randi Munn

Camera and Lenses by Panavision
Colour by Technicolor
Video Facility 4MC/Digital Magic
Sound by Sony Pictures Studios, Culver City,
California
Bryce Zabel Productions Inc. In association
with Columbia Pictures Television.

First Series Production Credits

Executive Producer : Bryce Zabel
Executive Producer : James D. Parriott
Created by : Bryce Zabel and
Brent V. Friedman
Producer : Brad Markowitz
Supervising Producer : Steve Aspis (except
Inhuman Nature, Hostile
Convergence, We Shall
Overcome, The Warren
Omission)
Supervising Producer : Brent V. Friedman
Supervising Producer : Steve Beers
Co-Producers : Bernie Laramie
Mark R. Schilz
Assistant Producer : Robert Parigi
Director of Photography : Steve Yaconelli ASC
Production Design : Curtis A. Schnell (All

except Hostile
Convergence and The
Warren Omission)
Greg Melton (Hostile
Convergence and The
Warren Omission)
Film Editor : Troy T. Takari
(Moving Targets, Ancient
Future, Dreamland, We
Shall Overcome, The
Enemy Within)
James Coblentz
(Mercury Rising,
Inhuman Nature, The
Last Wave)
Andrew Cohen (Dark
Day's Night)

Film Editor : Lou Angelo (*Hostile Convergence, The Warren Omission*)

Composer : Michael Hoenig

Unit Production Manager : Mark R Schilz

1st Assistant Director : James Dillon (*Moving Targets, Dreamland, Hostile Convergence, The Last Wave*)
Chris Stoia (*Mercury Rising*)
Richard Graves (*Dark Day's Night*)
John Slosser (*Ancient Future, Inhuman Nature, We Shall Overcome, The Enemy Within, The Warren Omission*)

2nd Assistant Director : Bob Kozicki

Casting : Robert J Ulrich CSA
Eric Dawson CSA
Carol Kritzer CSA

Costumes : Darryl LeVine

Post-Production : Jack Mongan

Camera Operator : David Parrish

Script Supervisor : Randa Rai Slack (except *Hostile Convergence* and *The Last Wave*)
Rhonda Hyde (*Hostile Convergence, The Last Wave*)

Production Sound Mixer : Thomas E. Allen CSA

Gaffer : Rich Sands

Key Grip : Frank Keever

Art Director : Michael Fox (*Moving Targets, Mercury Rising, Dark Day's Night, Ancient Future, Dreamland, Inhuman Nature, The Enemy Within*)
Colin Irwin (*Hostile Convergence, The Last Wave, We Shall Overcome, The Warren Omission*)

Set : Crista Schneider

Props Master : Brad Breitbach

Casting Assistant : Shawn Dawson

Make-up : John Rizzo

Production Accountant : Hilton Smith

Key Hair : Andrea Mizushima Jones

Transportation : Steve Hellerstein

Special Effects Co-ordinator : Larry Fioritto

Stunts Co-ordinator : John Moio

Location : Gary Kessell (*Moving Targets, Ancient Future, Dreamland, Hostile Convergence, The Last Wave, The Enemy Within*)
Larry Pearson (*Mercury Rising, Dark Day's Night, Inhuman Nature, We Shall Overcome, The Warren Omission*)

Production Co-ordinator : Ingrid K. Lohne

Assistant Production Co-ordinator : Stacy Radford

Script Co-ordinator : Adam Sigel

Assistant Editor : Bill Weinman (*Moving Targets, Dreamland, We Shall Overcome, The Enemy Within*)
Marilyn Adams (*Mercury Rising, Ancient Future, Inhuman Nature, The Last Wave*)
Jeff Hodge (*Dark Day's Night*)
Angie Brodar (*Hostile Convergence, The Warren Omission*)

Music Editor : Marty Wereski

Sound Supervisor : William Dotson

Sound Effects : Dave A Davis (*Moving Targets, Mercury Rising, Dark Day's Night, Ancient Future, Dreamland, Inhuman Nature*)
Mark Larry (*Hostile Convergence, The Last Wave, We Shall Overcome, The Enemy Within, The Warren Omission*)

Re-recording Mixers : Neil Brody
Gary Rodgers
Mike Olman

AREA 51 VISUAL EFFECTS CREW

Visual Effects Producer : Tim McHugh
Supervising Animator : Wayne England
(Moving Targets)
Karl Denham
(Mercury Rising,
Dreamland)
David Jones (Dark
Day's Night, Ancient
Future, Inhuman Nature,
Hostile Convergence,
The Last Wave)
Visual Effects
Co-ordinator : Sheri Rycus Weston
CGI Animators : Karl Denham (Moving
Targets, Ancient Future)
Andrew Harlow
(Moving Targets,
Mercury Rising,
Dreamland, Inhuman
Nature, Hostile
Convergence, The Last
Wave, Ancient Future)
Sheri Rycus Weston
(Moving Targets)
Justin Hammond
(Mercury Rising,

Dark Day's Night)
David Jones (Mercury
Rising, Hostile
Convergence)
Scott Wheller
(Mercury Rising)
Wayne England (We
Shall Overcome, The
Enemy Within)

Todd Masters
Company Crew : Greg Johnson
John Shea
Bernhard Eichholz
Thomas D. Bacho Jr.
Gloria Munez
Jaremy Aiello
Dave Matherly
(except The Last Wave,
The Enemy Within and
The Warren Omission)
William Fosh
Tim Huizing

Effects Production
Co-ordinator : Kristine Morgan
Assistant to Producer : Barbara Whiting
Stacy Koster
Umberto Autore Jr.
Julia Bent (The Last
Wave and The Warren
Omission only)

FURTHER READING

Berliner, Don and Friedman, Stanton. *Crash at Corona: The U.S. Military Retrieval and Cover-Up of a UFO.* Paragon House, 1992

Davies, Paul. *Are We Alone?: Philosophical Implications of the Discovery of Extraterrestrial Life.* Simon & Schuster, 1992

Fawcett, Lawrence & Greenwood, Barry J. *The UFO Cover-Up: What the Government Won't Say.* Simon & Schuster, 1992.

Good, Timothy. *Above Top Secret: The Worldwide UFO Cover-Up.* William Morrow & Company, Inc., 1988

Good, Timothy. *Beyond Top Secret: The Worldwide UFO Security Threat. With a foreword by Admiral of the Fleet, The Lord Hill-Norton GCB.* Sidgwick & Jackson, an imprint of Macmillan Publishers Ltd., 1996

Manchester, William. *The Glory and the Dream. A Narrative History of America. 1932 – 1972.* Bantam Books, 1975

Randle, Kevin D. & Schmitt, Donald R. *The Truth About the UFO Crash at Roswell.* M. Evans & Company, Inc., 1994.

Spencer, John. *The UFO Encyclopedia.* Avon Books, 1991.

Steiger, Bred, Ed. *Project Blue Book.* Ballantine Books, 1976.